BEACHES

100 ULTIMATE ESCAPES

BEACHES
100 ULTIMATE ESCAPES

Edited by Sabrina Talarico with Stefano Passaquindici

UNIVERSE

INTRODUCTION

First islands, then beaches. Both symbolize dreams, poetry, travel literature. This second volume in the 100 Ultimate Escapes series published by Rizzoli RCS in collaboration with the GIST (Gruppo Italiano Stampa Turistica) journalists is dedicated entirely to the beaches—be they silky and sandy, pebbly, white or pink, wide or narrow, volcanic or coral, short or miles long. Some are in the Caribbean, in the middle of the ocean, in the legendary seas of the East, or floating in the deep, cold waters of the West. Others teeter on the edge of a continent or perch on a lagoon.

When it comes to choosing a seaside vacation, it is the presence, distance, dimensions, and characteristics of the beach you're going to that make all the difference. It's no coincidence that vacation companies and hotels spend a lot of time describing them in great detail in their brochures and on their websites, each adjective carefully chosen and judged. This is because there is no greater disappointment for a vacationer than to arrive at their destination and find a beach that fails to live up to their expectations.

Beaches and, of course, the seas around them really can make or break a vacation. This publication offers descriptions of each one of the 100 beaches we've chosen from around the world: the United Kingdom, France, Italy, Spain, Mexico, Chile, the United States, Israel, Yemen, India, Vietnam, Kenya, New Zealand, Polynesia, Tasmania, and beyond.

For convenience sake, we've followed the lead of our previous book on the world's top 100 islands and divided our beaches into six categories. Each one will act as a guide for the reader: we've crammed all the dancing, drinking, and dining into the **Fun** beaches section while the **Unreachable** beaches are places that offer incredible solitude and tranquility. The **Legendary** beaches have earned their status because of their historic value or, shall we say, services to the movie industry. With the **Natural Paradises** section, respect for the environment and delicate local ecosystems really is the order of the day. Continuing that theme, the **Protected** beaches are all carefully monitored by government or international institutions to ensure that the very characteristics that make them so unique are maintained. On a much lighter note, the **Sports** beaches are the places to go if you're competitive at all and like a challenge, be it ashore, in the sky, or, of course, on and in the water.

Each one of these beaches has at least one feature that makes it special. On Bangaram Beach, in the Laccadives, you can feast on tandoori chicken or fried shrimp as you wander barefoot along its length. At Pwani Mchangani (Zanzibar), you'll see the local ladies cultivating seaweed as they have done for a hundred years or more. Pampelonne in France first shot to fame with Brigitte Bardot and is now a favorite haunt of both Robert De Niro and Jack Nicholson; in Jimbaran Bay (Bali), each evening you'll see men and women dressed in elegant silk saris leaving arrangements of flowers and incense in thanks to the ocean for its generosity. Los Cabos Arch in

Mexico is known as the Love and Divorce Beach because on the one side it is calm and on the other tempestuous. Utah Beach in Normandy, France, has gone down in history because of the D-Day landings during World War II, while Venice Beach (USA) is a vibrant haven for everything from punks to hippies, celebrities, artists, and bankers. Bahía Gardner (Galápagos) is populated by pelicans, Darwin finches, and iguanas. Each evening on Cua Dai beach in Vietnam, vacationers watch the spectacle of the local fishing boats sailing out to lamp octopuses and shrimp from the comfort of cushions arranged on the sand. In the Andaman Islands, The Beach is carpeted by star-like jasmine whose sweet, delicate, yet poignant scent fills the air, while the sand on Tuscany's Cala Violina beach is so incredibly fine that when you walk barefoot over it, it makes a violin-like sound. Puri in India is an attraction for locals and dotted with little kiosks selling sweet tea and coconut milk.

Some of the beaches we feature don't really have a name as such—particularly if they are on an island or an atoll. That's the case with Francisqui, a small beach/island that's part of the Los Roques archipelago in Venezuela. A magical world, a palette of unparalleled colors. We also describe the seas that lap these beaches, the waves that crash over them and reshape them, and the people that live on them, their festivals and rituals. We discuss the areas inland from them as well, the countries, regions, and towns that surround them.

Once again we've called upon the services of a considerable number of GIST journalists and photographers who've contributed their own personal experiences and knowledge to create a volume aimed at focusing not on the world's 100 most beautiful beaches but its most singular and significant ones. Beaches that, for whatever reason, you really do have to see at least once in your lifetime.

That meant a lot of work: coordinating texts and deadlines for 63 different journalists, all very busy and often traveling themselves, really did put my proverbial patience to the test at times. But in the end we did what we set out to do and the result has more than rewarded our efforts.

A very special word of thanks to **Marco Ausenda**, head of Rizzoli Libri, who suggested doing this second "100" volume to GIST; and also to all the GIST journalists and photographers who worked with me and made their own invaluable contributions. My gratitude to **Franco Barbagallo**, who coordinated the work of all these excellent photographers, and to **Ada Mascheroni**, who contributed with her usual good grace and generosity of spirit. So did we leave any beaches out? Yes, probably, and for that we apologize. But every choice means compromise. Yet, to take a positivist view, every choice is also useful and productive as well. Meanwhile, our voyage of discovery continues to other islands, other beaches, other seas, and other destinations.

Sabrina Talarico

TABLE OF CONTENTS

Natural paradises

Sports beaches

Unreachable beaches

Cannon Beach

Love and Divorce Beach

Venice Beach

Waikiki

Waimea Bay

South Beach

Playa Blanca

Cabbage Beach

Shroud Cay

Grand Plage

Cabarete

Bayahibe

Seven Mile Beach

Jhonny Cay

Poneloya

Playa Tamarindo

Manihi

Arrecifes

Rabida

Bahía Gardner

Anakena Beach

Francisqui

Saline

Anse de Mays

Palmetto Point

Grande Anse des Salines

Morro de Areia

Jericoacoara

Genipabù

Praia do Gunga

Praia do Forte

Copacabana

Ipanema

Punta Pirulil

Caleta Valdés

Zlatni Rat

Acciaroli, Ieranto

Venice Lido

Tylösand

Le Touquet

Promenade des Planches, Utah Beach

Brighton

Elie

Burton Bradstock

Marina di Ravenna

Cape de la Hague

Belles Rives, Pampelonne

La Double

Saleccia

En Vau

Girolata

Playa de la Barceloneta

Cala Mitjiana

Piscinas, Spiaggia Rosa

Cala Saona

Is Arutas

Cala d'Arena

Cala Violina

Castelfusano

Cala Cinque Denti

Torre Salsa

Ramla Bay

Beriknica

Praia Pombas

Clifton Beach

Super Paradise

Golden Beach

Hayarkon Street Beach

Coral Bay

Jumeirah Beach

Bálos

Mangrove Beach

Chowpatty

Púri

Qalansya

Ngapali Beach

Om Beach

Marina Beach

Hat Sai Kaew

Cua Dai

Bangaram

Dayang Bunting

Anse Latio

The Beach

Che Chale

Diani Beach

Pwani Mchangani

Jimbaran Bay

Aitutaki

Belle Mare

Cape Range

Heron Island

Le Morne

Goukamma

Bondi Beach

Wineglass Bay

Say goodbye to peace and quiet. Even sunbathing is out. These fun beaches have everything else, though: massages, buggy rides, happy hour, fitness, and dancing 'til dawn. Take a samba course or let your body flow to the sultry rhythms of reggae. These are not the beaches to go to if you need to relax or spend time on your own. They will, however, hit the spot if you're looking for a massive energy boost, pure fun, and maybe some wild barefoot dancing in the sand. Cocktails, glamour, chic parties, and a hot nightlife: you'll be entranced by the atmosphere of a never-ending summer. Start north and work your way south or vice versa... but wherever you go you'll be surrounded by the magical beauty of nature as you explore these havens of fun in the sun.

Carmen Rolle

FUN
beaches

BRAZIL

COPACABANA
RIO DE JANEIRO

NEARBY

Start your visit to Rio with the **Pão de Açúcar** (Sugarloaf), one of the city's trademark sites. Take a ride in Brazil's first cable car, which also takes you to another legendary Rio landmark, the 100-foot-high *Cristo Redentor* gazing out over the city from the Corcovado (2,200 ft.). A stroll along the **Dias Ferreira** will lead you to the city's newest stores. The 0.4-mile-long street is packed with restaurants, workshops, showrooms, designer boutiques, bookshops, cafés, chocolate-makers, and tearooms. Round off your day by exploring Rio's luxury shopping streets: Visconde de Pirajá, Barão da Torre, Garcia d'Ávila, and Aníbal de Mendonça.

T o the rest of the world, the melting-pot of Copacabana Beach is very much the symbol par excellence of the nation of Brazil.

The view from the Sugarloaf sweeps across the "luminous, blue beach," as its name translates from the Quiche language. The colors are stunning: the deep blue of the Baia di Rio, the endless expanse of shimmering sand, the unmistakable skyline. The most famous building is the Copacabana Palace, a charming tropical belle époque creation and very much an icon of Rio in its heyday as the *cidade maravilhosa* during the early decades of the 1900s. This was a golden era for a city that was actually the capital of Brazil from 1763 to 1960. "Ao sol de Copacabana," to borrow a verse from poet Vinicius de Moraes, the fun begins early and never stops.

This beach is perfect at any hour. There is a very direct relationship with the sea and, more than anything else, Copacabana beach is the symbol of Rio itself, its beach culture, and its talent for trend-setting in everything from music to games and fashion. Restaurants, casinos, and bars light up the night in a joyous cacophony of color and sound. This is a city of samba and carnival, a place where fun and legend intermingle in the shade of the Copacabana Palace.

Copacabana is where Rio residents get together. It's a huge sensual open space throbbing with life. It may not be Rio's most stunning beach, but without a doubt, it's a stopover for tourists and beloved by the locals. There is the Avenida Atlantica, with its wonderfully undulated stone pattern that echoes the shapes of the waves out at sea. Arriving from Botafogo and from Leme beach, the incredibly long Rio shore washes up on the golden sands of Copacabana. It is here, to the soundtrack of the snarling traffic on the Avenida Atlantica behind it, that the Copacabana legend is reborn each and every day.

Above: Copacabana Beach, with brilliant colors. **Opposite:** *The Avenida Atlantica and the waterfront hug the length of the gleaming white sandy beach.*

GENIPABÙ
RIO GRANDE DO NORTE

If you follow the coast 18 miles from Natal in northeast Brazil, you'll reach Genipabù beach in the city of Extremoz—State of Rio Grande do Norte. It's famous for its huge sand dunes, beautiful lakes, and, of course, the *mangues*. These are mangrove swamps, home to countless crabs that come out of hiding at sunset. The countryside is also dotted by innumerable *taipa* houses built from a mix of wood and clay, and also *sapê* or grass-roofed huts. These all blend in wonderfully with the surrounding coconut palms. Near the beach there are plenty of *pousadas*, family-run inns that also serve great seafood, like lobsters and shrimp. After all, this is Brazil's prime seafood production area.

The biggest local attraction, however, is the Genipabù Dune Park, a spectacular and ever-changing expanse of sand dunes that extends from behind the village of the same name over a massive 2,895 acres and is home to a wonderfully diverse array of flora and fauna as well as unique areas of the Mata Atlântica or Atlantic Forest. The sand dunes, which can be up to 160 feet in height, are at the mercy of the dry wind that blows in from the

NEARBY

"Move like a wave and breathe the purest area in all the Americas" declare the posters adorning the waterfront at **Punta Negra**, the stunning bay slumbering gently at the foot of Natal, the "vacation capital" of northeast Brazil. And there's nothing easier to do in this little corner of paradise. Abandon yourself to the warm, sensual rhythm of Brazilian music and you'll find yourself flowing along like a wave on the sea. Take a big deep breath and you'll feel purged of the city smog. It truly is vacation time all year round in Natal. Actually, it's a way of life here, so try it out and see if it's right for you!

Above: Enjoying a drink and the sea view after a dune buggy race. Left: The huge Genipabù sand dunes reach all the way to the sea. Opposite: A traditional pousada on the sandy promontory of Genipabù.

Atlantic, which sculpts and re-sculpts them, trimming them, piling them up, and moving them around like some whimsical sculptor might.

There are several ways to explore the dunes. It all depends on how adventurous you want to be. You can try a camel ride—something that kids love—or decide to hike your way. If you're feeling particularly sporty or adventurous you can rent an ultralight or a dune buggy, the latter with four-wheel drive, making it exceptional for the park. It's a truly unforgettable experience. Before tackling the dunes, the *bugueiros,* or professional buggy drivers, always ask their passengers if they want a ride *con emocao* (high adrenaline). If you opt for this then be prepared to find yourself roaring down white sandy banks dozens of feet high at angles of almost 90 degrees. The dune buggy won't stop, it'll just go into free-fall. The result is an incredible adrenaline rush. Taking a camel ride is a little more laid back, to say the least, and although it doesn't offer quite the exhilaration of a buggy, it is one of the most unique tourist options available in Rio Grande do Norte.

If you don't suffer from vertigo, then you'll love the dizzying views of the north beach from the comfort of one of the ultralights flying out of Genipabù. You'll soar over white sandy beaches along the coast, clear blue sea, lagoons, and bright green coconut palms.

Kids of all ages will adore trying their skills at *Aerobunda*, a sort of rudimentary version of bungee jumping into the Jacumã lagoon, which involves sitting in a leather seat attached to steel cables and being pushed off the top of an enormous dune directly into the water. One way of cooling down!

However, if you prefer keeping your feet firmly on the ground or even under a table, you can savor the delights of fresh grilled lobster and shrimp kebabs sold from stands at the top of the dunes. Genipabù doesn't just have a beautiful blue sea: it also has sun, the tastes, smells, colors, and spellbinding magic of Brazil itself.

Opposite: *Genipabù Beach's sandy expanse crisscrossed by dune buggy tracks.* **Above**: *A camel patiently awaits his next passengers.* **Right**: *Stunning views around Genipabù.*

MORRO DE AREIA
BOA VISTA

Translated literally, Morro de Areia means "wall of sand." But this description doesn't really do justice to the extraordinary spectacle of this sliver of the Sahara, which has been transplanted onto the island of Boa Vista, the nearest and possibly the most beautiful of the 10 Cape Verde Islands off the African mainland. Dunes stretch away over the horizon and slide into the sea, gently moved and reshaped by the Harmattan winds, which carry with them sand from the Sahara. It's a surreal, sculpted landscape, best enjoyed in the soft light of dawn, the glow of sunset, or by the unearthly gleam of a full moon. Nestled between the pristine Praia Varandinha and Praia di Chave, Morro de Areia's dunes also provide the venue for the gruelling 150 km, nonstop Boa Vista Ultramarathon, which takes place each December in these extraordinary surroundings. It is the test of endurance par excellence, according to participants.

Watersports lovers, however, will adore Boa Vista's fantastic waters and endless beaches. The trade winds blow here between November and May, making it perfect for wind and kite surfing. The locals claim that God, after Creation, rubbed his hands together in satisfaction and a few grains of dirt still clinging to the trades shook loose and fell into the sea, and the Cape Verde Islands were born. Today the islands remain a refuge of strength and beauty, providing a natural habitat for sea turtles and humpback whales. A treasure trove of volcanic rock and seashells are gently sculpted into bizarre shapes by the powerful undertow. This is a lush green oasis dotted with tiny villages. There's even the wreck of a beached freighter, now home to a romantic pair of sea eagles. "Boa vista!" was the exultant cry uttered by the first Portuguese sailors who gazed upon this lovely island, and saw a small paradise on earth.

NEARBY

Located on the island's northwestern coast, the capital town of **Sal Rei** still has some low colonial-style Portuguese houses and commercial buildings in the old port that bear witness to a glorious past. Ships once moored here to load up royal quality salt, which was exported until the end of the 19th century. Don't miss the main square, which is where everyone gathers. It's also home to the market and the **Church of Santa Isabel**. Kids dive into the water at the **Alfândega** or the old customs house and fishermen drag their colorful fishing boats out of the water here. Facing this section of town is the **Ilhéu de Sal Rei** and the ruins of the 19th-century **Duque de Bragança** fort, built to protect the village from pirate raids.

Above: Fishing takes on a whole new meaning in the seas around the Cape Verde Islands. Opposite. The huge sand dune lining the seashore at Boa Vista.

SUPER PARADISE
MYKONOS

NEARBY

Mykonos is the undisputed Aegean capital of fun. No vacation here would be complete without a visit to the port, which is overlooked by the elegant Hora, the oldest part of the town. Here fishing trawlers and luxury yachts sail in beautifully colored waters. One of Hora's most attractive quarters is lively Little Venice, where the nightlife starts at sunset. Abandon yourself to the sound of the waves as you sip a glass of ouzo. Don't miss the views of the island from the **Kato Myli** windmills on the promontory to the southwest of Little Venice. Some are former restaurants now used as tourist lodgings.

Mykonos is party central of the Greek Islands. It's a truly irreverent, carnal, fun place. The moment you step outside the airport you feel as though you've entered a parallel world with a cosmopolitan vibe unlike anything else.

Whipped by the cool, northeast Meltemi wind in summer, this barren little island attracts vacationers from all over the world. Sun, sea, and fun are the three driving forces of a vacation on Mykonos. The island has beaches of all kinds and for all tastes. But for the real action, you'll have to head south in the direction of the Paradise and Super Paradise Beaches. Paradise, with its rough sand and shingle stretches, is the first fun stopover point. During the day this is a tranquil place to bask in the sun, but then between late afternoon and evening it becomes a pleasure palace, thanks to one of the island's most famous and loudest hangouts, the Tropicana. The atmosphere there is hot, hot, hot and Tropicana certainly lives up to its name. The music is deafening and booms out full-blast for hours into the evening air. Everything and anything goes.

Super Paradise is right nearby and is set in a rocky bay. You'll have to cross steep, narrow roads to get here. The beach seems straight out of a fairy tale: a slice of heaven on earth lapped by the incredible blue waters of the Aegean. Super Paradise is a long stretch of fine white sand, which turns a wonderful gold in the evening sun. Dotted with sun umbrellas, *tavernas*, and beach bars selling cocktails to the thirsty, it booms with music day and night. This really is a Super Paradise for hedonists, particularly if you come here with an openmind, ready to embrace anything the day or night may bring.

*Above: The windmills at Kato Myl in Mykonos. **Opposite**: Super Paradise Beach, the great symbol of Mykonos at its wildest and most fun.*

CHOWPATTY
MAHARASHTRA

Anyone coming to Chowpatty Beach looking for somewhere to do a little sun worshipping or swimming will be disappointed. Mumbai's most famous beach runs along the north of Marine Drive, and is really more the city's melting pot, attracting people of all ages and castes. It's much quieter during the day and really only comes into its own in the evenings. This is when the locals come out for a stroll and to enjoy the cooling temperatures (relatively speaking by local standards). They come here too, of course, in an attempt to escape from the noise and chaos of a city of 17 million. Most of all, though, they come for the carnival atmosphere that lights up the beach each night. Sunset is a good time to arrive: you can feast your eyes on the empty horizon and be caressed by the sea breeze as the sun plunges into the Arabian Sea, and on the lights that have earned Marine Drive the nickname of Queen's Necklace. If you choose to watch the spectacle unfold from the comfort of the terraces of one of the elegant hotels lining the drive, you will be left with some unforgettable memories. Just sit back, relax, and soak up the atmosphere. Then take a stroll down the beach itself. This is where it all happens: you'll see contortionists in excruciating poses, monkeys and their trainers, fortune tellers, and people offering pony and camel rides. If you're feeling hungry, try the coconut milk and *bhelpuri*, a delicious local snack made of puffed rice, vegetables, tomatoes, and boiled potatoes doused in green pepper chutney and scooped up with *puri*, a type of Indian fried bread. The mouth-watering local food is all part of the experience. Treat yourself to a vigorous head massage from one of the expert *malishwallahs*. If you happen to come to Chowpatty Beach in August or September, you'll see the Hindu festival of Ganesh Chaturthi. This major event attracts enormous crowds who come to venerate the effigies of the elephant-headed god of good fortune carried in procession through the city streets before being immersed in the sea.

NEARBY

Mumbai, the world's second largest city after Shanghai, is the commercial heart of India. It is relatively new and its colonial architecture is one of its main attractions. These include the **Gateway of India**, an arch built to commemorate the visit of King George V and Queen Mary, and the **Victoria Terminus**, a railway station with a cathedral-like neo-gothic façade—well worth a visit. Another gothic masterpiece is the covered **Crawford Market**, to which the people of Mumbai flock each day to buy their produce. To get a good idea of contemporary Indian art, don't miss the **National Gallery of Modern Art,** which also has temporary shows.

Opposite: Vendors of local snacks standing at their stall on Chowpatty Beach. **Left:** *A view from above looking down onto Chowpatty Beach as sunset begins.*

A red kite flies high in the violet light of dusk. Others drift up to join it, fierce dragons battling with each other to fly the highest and farthest. The sunset glow suffuses Jimbaran Beach like a gentle golden rain as the tide gently recedes. The pace of the day slows as children play ball while the last rays of the sun glitter in the puddles left by the retreating sea. The wind ruffles the distant waves while tourists trawl the clusters of *warungs* (local Balinese restaurants) that dot the white crescent of Jimbaran, in search of the best lobster. There's always a lot of haggling going on outside the fish tanks as their occupants tread water, blissfully unaware of the fate that awaits them. The colorful *warung* tables and chairs gleam in the fading light of dusk, and dinner seems the perfect excuse to sit back and watch the sun gently sliding beneath the horizon. But this is also the time of day when the locals make their votive offerings. You'll see the same processions every evening as small arrangements of incense and flowers are left on the water's edge by men and women in elegant silk *sarongs* in thanks to the ocean for its generosity. Earlier in the afternoon a long procession crossed the beach, a lengthy line of people bearing aloft effigies of Barong, a half-dog, half-lion creature symbolizing good, and Randa, a terrifying witch, who are locked in a never-ending struggle. The sun is now a fiery ball and tumbling gently into the ocean leaving splinters of gold, orange, cerise, and pink on the surface of the sea while the dusk-tinted clouds glide by with ease and grace. Soon the light will drain out of the sky altogether, but for now the sand is wet and there are still a few women here and there selling fish. As they do everyday, they've each set up little stands at the water's edge. They'll be back again tomorrow when the fishermen arrive with their catch: the gift of the great, generous ocean.

NEARBY

The very center of international surfing in Bali lies to the south of Jimbaran. Dotted around the lofty, atmospheric 11th-century temple of **Pura Luhur Ulu Watu** are the legendary breakpoints that surfers all over the globe seek. You'll also find plenty of little guest houses and *warung* selling, renting, and repairing surfboards, and offering food, drinks, and massages. The only area you can swim problem-free is at **Pantai Suluban**. You can also see the surrounding bays and watch stunning sunsets from the cliff there as well. Another must-see, preferably at sundown, is **Tanah Lot** and its breathtaking temple.

Above: Dinner tables at the water's edge with perfect sunset views.
Opposite: A group of locals takes part in a religious procession at Jimbaran Bay.

HAYARKON BEACH
TEL AVIV

From the 20th story of the hotel, the huge, sandy, empty length of Hayarkon Street Beach stretches away into emptiness broken only here and there by a tidy cluster of closed sun umbrellas. The sea is calm, clear, and a gorgeous blue-green. We are in Tel Aviv, a youthful, eclectic city right in the very heart of Israel. Hayarkon Street is all about fun and sports. This is where the city's residents come to sunbathe, play, work out, drink exotic beverages, have dinner, and listen to music. But first thing in the morning, Hayarkon Street Beach is an oasis of quiet and order. Only a few people stroll along the shore, while some arrive with their own sun umbrellas and stretch out on the sand.

Later in the afternoon, the atmosphere changes as the beach gradually fills up with a wonderful mix of people—young, old, families with kids, hippies, students, white collar workers in suits and ties. Soccer, volleyball, and rugby games start up. Others play cards or smoke the *narghilè* or use the outdoor gyms. Bars and restaurants set gazebos, tables, and chairs on the sand itself.

The Israeli nightlife is about to begin and thousands of tourists and locals alike get together and eat, drink, dance, and have fun. These night owls move from the beaches at Rothschild Boulevard, Albert Square, and Neve Zedek—an old quarter that's now very trendy—to Sheinkin Street to the old port of Ashod, where there are dozens of restaurants, coffee shops, wine bars, discos, theaters, bistros, art galleries, and kosher restaurants. Hayarkon Street Beach, and all the others besides, are the hub of Tel Aviv, a genuinely tolerant melting pot of young, old, Jew and Arab, men, women, gays and lesbians.

NEARBY

There's a lot to see in a city as ancient and eclectic as Tel Aviv: **Carmel Market** is a large open-air fruit and produce market; **Nahalat Binyamin** is a pedestrianized street that hosts a handicraft market every Friday and Tuesday; the "White City" is also a World Heritage Site thanks to its 1,000-plus Bauhaus buildings (don't miss the **Bauhaus Museum**). Of course, you have to take in Jaffa, too, the original part of the town, the port of **Ashod**. And don't miss the now-renovated old quarter of **Neve Zedek**, which is home to Rokach House, built in 1887 for the first settlement of Jews on this stretch of coastline.

*Above: Young people, intellectuals, and sports enthusiasts of all ethnicities and nationalities share the beach in complete harmony. **Right:** Games and hangouts along the waterfront.*

MARINA DI RAVENNA
EMILIA-ROMAGNA

Marina di Ravenna is the trendy melting pot beach on the Riviera Romagnola. For years it has been a place where people come to meet, socialize, and do sports, where anything and everything can happen. The clear blue sea is a plus. It has, in fact, revolutionized beach life in Italy. At sunset, crowds gather to sip drinks and dance against a backdrop of pine woods and dunes: this is happy hour, Italian style. It all began in 1994 when at the Duna degli Orsi swimming pool/beach club, throngs of hippy-chic, fit youngsters began spontaneously hanging out on the beach, drinking and dancing until dawn. By the end of the 1990s Marina di Ravenna had become beach party central; these gatherings gradually replaced nightclubs and put the beach right back at the heart of the action. Marina di Ravenna is Romagna's biggest beach and is backed by pine woods, dunes, and salt water lagoons. There are no skyscrapers or hotels here, and the views to the north are of Ravenna's industrial and port districts. But none of that seems to matter.

Sport is another big source of fun there, too. Surfers thank their lucky stars for Marina di Ravenna as it is one of the few good spots for catching waves on Italy's northeast coast. The beach is about 1,000 feet wide, and you'll have to cross extremely busy beach tennis courts to reach the sea for a bathe. In recent years, the Duna degli Orsi has offered an impressive lineup of events dedicated to encounters and dinners with famous authors. There are 42 similar swimming pool/beach clubs at Marina di Ravenna and many organize wine tastings and other kinds of courses. In summer though, the goal is always fun, fun, fun.

NEARBY

Visit the city of Ravenna itself: **San Vitale, Theodoric's Mausoleum**, the lovely basilica of **Sant'Apollinare in Classe** just outside the city. Bikes are the best form of transportation. The **Po Delta National Park** includes the **Oasi di Boscoforte** and, farther to the south, the ancient salt mines of **Cervia**. The town of Cervia also has an atmospheric main piazza. In **Milano Marittima**, check out the designer shopping on **Viale Gramsci**. It also has numerous street bars. Don't miss the Riviera's most famous night club, **Pineta**.

*Above: Papeete stirs up the evening fun on the beach. **Opposite**: Young Italians dance their hearts out.*

SEVEN MILE BEACH
WESTMORELAND

Seven Mile Beach has made Long Bay at Negril in the northeast of the island of Jamaica famous. Visitors flock here from all over the globe to vacation in the Caribbean sunshine and soak up the festive atmosphere. There's still something slightly transgressive and nonconformist about the place, too, a hangover from the 1960s and '70s, when hippies came here in search of *ganja* (marijuana), free love, and an alternative lifestyle. They were helped on their journey by a coast road built at the end of the 1950s. Before then what's now fun central was just a small fishing village in an area reachable only by sea because of the Great Morass marshlands, a former refuge of 18th-century pirates when the island was under British rule. The past is everywhere in Jamaica as are the ghosts of the celebrities who made it famous, from Hollywood greats like Errol Flynn, who had a home here, to Ian Fleming, who wrote his James Bond novels here. The list is topped, of course, by the late, great Bob Marley—the air is filled with reggae music, particularly at night in Negril. There is 24-hour action at Long Bay, along Seven Mile Beach and Norman Manley Boulevard, which runs parallel to it. By day, it's all about the sea as vacationers swim in crystalline waters, waterski, and windsurf. Diving and snorkeling in the marvelous coral reef brings you face-to-face with octopuses, sea starfish, turtles, and, if you're lucky, a few nurse sharks making their rounds of the many wrecks littering the ocean floor. The beach is lined with resorts, and there are usually craftspeople selling their carved wooden products. Sun umbrellas and loungers are all part of the landscape too, but there are still completely wild areas of coast broken up by maritime brush and mangroves. Happy hour reveals the stunning beauty of the Jamaican sunsets. As evening falls, the restaurants fill up and the smells of the spicy local specialties drift out into the air, the live music bars open their doors, the rum begins to flow, and the dancing goes on until dawn. Absolutely magical! Try it and see. You won't be disappointed.

NEARBY

In the center of Negril, there's a roundabout with three main roads leading off of it. Take the West End Road, which runs 3 miles south along the coast and leads to the cliffs. Just before the Negril Point Lighthouse (1894), stop off at **Rick's Café**. Immortalized in a host of films including *How Stella Got Her Groove Back*, it has become something of a mecca for tourists as a temple to Negril's good life. As you wait for sundown, you can watch the local youngsters doing wonderfully acrobatic diving. Nature-lovers shouldn't miss a trip to the **Ys Falls** and the **Royal Palm Reserve** at the edge of the **Great Morass**.

Above: A stretch of beach at Long Bay with tropical vegetation behind it.
Opposite: The fine white sand of the tourist beach at Long Bay look inviting indeed.

CHE CHALE
MALINDI

At Che Chale, 7 miles north of Malindi, the wind shapes the dunes while the blisteringly hot African sun makes the sand glitter like gold for a good 17 miles. At sunset, it looks like a huge expanse of red-gold embroidery. The clouds seem to race along under the waves while local men and women trawl the sand for clams and other shellfish, the leftovers of a silent life that springs up along the seashore. Farther on, beyond the white foam of the waves, slender wooden boats glide along. Children play in the water along the shore. Their skin gleams like silk, their smiles are iridescently beautiful, and their wonderful joie de vivre shines in their eyes. You can bike along the shore, too. Or if you're looking for something faster, try a camel, a quad bike, or an off-roader.

To the east, the Sabaki-Galana river flows into the ocean: there the red waters, swollen with earth, unfold lazily and gently down to the sea. If you're lucky, you might even get to see some hippos chilling out in its depths. The huge expanses of salt water attract hundreds of pink flamingoes as well. This is a windy spot and there are always a few kite surfers gliding along the water. Your feet will sink into the sandy dunes as you make your way into the lush vegetation ringing the beach. The gilded, windy Che Chale is particularly beautiful seen from above. Its wild sea changes with the tides and the light, images blurring and reforming time and time again. Stunning, like Kenya itself.

NEARBY

Make your way from Che Chale to **Mambrui**. At sunset each evening in this ancient Muslim village, the women cook on open fires. They make rice pilaf with vegetables, spices, and meat; *wali mweupe*, rice with coconut milk; *samaki wa nazi*, fish with coconut milk; *muhogo wa nazi*, cassava with coconut milk; *samaki wa kupaka*, grilled fish with spices; *kuku wa nazi*, chicken with coconut milk. The traditional mud and straw houses are painted with murals. There is a **16th-century Muslim burial ground** on the edge of the village. There a majestic baobab tree stands as a silent guard over the ancient tombs as the first shadows of evening fall.

Above: The reddish hues of the beach at Che Chale can be crossed by an off-roader. Great fun!
Right: Kite surfing is a very popular sport on the beach at Che Chale.

CALA SAONA
FORMENTERA

Cala Saona is an extraordinary natural paradise and one of Formentera's most famous beaches. A stunning crescent of cobalt blue water so beautiful you couldn't care less that it's jam packed with people during the summer months. It is found 3 miles from Sant Francesc Xavier, between Punta Rasa and Caló d'en Trull, near the eponymous village, on the southwest side of the island. Cala Saona beach is part of the Cap Alt Natural Park and lies in a deep inlet carved out between high cliffs that shelter it beautifully from the wind. It is a magnificent expanse of soft, white sand stretching around 500 feet and backing onto gentle dunes. The entire bay is also ringed by a shady pine forest. The sea is a brilliant turquoise with a sandy bottom that slopes away gently. Its depths are home to colonies of *posidonia*, a native Mediterranean seaweed essential for the marine habitat, making it perfect for swimming and long snorkeling stints.

Cala Saona is a very well-equipped beach: there is a tourist facility, various little seafront restaurants, and plenty of colorful *chiringuitos* (kiosks) from which visitors can admire the beautiful sunsets over cocktails to the melodic sounds of Spanish music. If you are exploring the island by scooter or bike, you can park free in the parking area near the beach.

The only building on the entire shore is the big Hotel Cala Saona. The whole area around the beach is charming, too: there are numerous little roads running south along the coast with paths leading from them into lush shady pines and maritime brush—perfect spots to chill out for a while or enjoy a picnic out of the hot sun. You'll be surrounded by quite beautiful sand dunes.

Another plus of this section of the coast is the marvelous views from its beaches. They afford truly magical Mediterranean sunsets—another great excuse to enjoy a cocktail or

NEARBY

Don't miss the magnificent sunsets over the bay. They're even better seen from on high—try the *chiringuito* where Juan Ribas makes wonderfully delicious cocktails: piña coladas, caipirinhas, caipiroska. The hospitality is warm and typical of the entire island. Perch yourself on the rocks or at one of Juan's little tables, and wile away an hour or so picking out the sphinx-like shapes of the islands of **Es Vedrá** and **Es Vedranell** in the distance, or just feasting your eyes on the lush hills of southern Ibiza. On very clear days, you should even be able to catch sight of the craggy peaks around **Deniá** on the mainland.

*Opposite: A stretch of coastline on Formentera, a flat, sandy island. **Left**: The sea at Cala Saona; a lot of vacationers anchor their boats near the beach and then come ashore for the famous sunset cocktail hour.*

two on the beach before dinner. Not an experience you'll forget in a hurry. Even getting there is fun as you'll pass through some magnificent countryside. From Sant Francesc Xavier, follow the signs for Cala Saona, south of the capital. After just over 1 mile, you'll come to a junction. The road heading west will get you to the coast. There are plenty of signs for the sea but if you have any doubts at all, just follow the music from the *chiringuitos*. If you're traveling by car, take the long road straight ahead, with gorgeous rust-colored fields filled with carob and fig trees and pine groves. Then, after around 2 miles, the truly magical sight of Cala Saona bay will open up before your eyes.

Above: *The waters around the Balearics are crystal clear, excellent for snorkeling.*
Right: *A view of Cala Saona beach from the pine forest behind it.*

PLAYA DE LA BARCELONETA
CATALONIA

This is the nearest beach to Barcelona, Catalonia's cosmopolitan capital. Like the city, it is an open-minded, open-hearted multinational spot best summed up in the slogan *Barcelona oberta al mar*, which means "Barcelona open to the sea." Playa de la Barceloneta isn't the city's only beach but it is certainly the most representative. It consists of half a mile of sandy shore that runs from Carrer de l'Almirall Cervera to the Porto Olimpico and is very easy to get to either by public transport or on foot. The beach is popular with both locals and tourists alike in search of a bit of relaxation and fun. There are always people out on this stretch of sand, which takes its name from the former fishing quarter of Barceloneta, which was laid out at the start of the 18th century as a little Manhattan. You'll see businessmen, still in their suits, fleeing their stifling offices and the trade fairs at lunchtime. That's in the summer, but it's still a great place to come in winter and spring. At those times of the year, too, the light is incredible, especially around the narrow streets lined by tiny two-story fishermen's houses. The beach was opened up and denuded of almost all the kiosks that lined it in preparation for the 1992 Olympics. There are now just a few simple structures remaining: the stone sun loungers, the volleyball courts, bike parks and tracks, the skating area, a children's playground, and a well-equipped "beach center", which is open between June and September and offers a plethora of sports and seaside activities. You'll come across it just in front of the Hospital del Mar. Room has been made for art on the beach in the shape of permanent installations right along its length. *L'Estel Ferit* or *Wounded Star* is a pile of steel cubes made by sculptor Rebecca Horn on the beach itself while Frank Gehry's famous *Fish* is on the Port Olympic waterfront with the twin towers of the Hotel Arts, the chicest place in the area, behind it.

NEARBY

Visit **Negra y Criminal**, a small but brilliantly stocked specialist crime and procedural (*novela negra*) bookstore on Carrer del la Sal in Barceloneta. Another must-see in the area is **La Maquinista Terrestre y Marítima**, a former 19th-century iron foundry whose massive, roaring furnaces were coal-fired. Locomotives, boat engines, and metal bridges were all manufactured there. It's now something of a monument to industrial architecture, and photovoltaic panels provide an attractive contrast to the smokestacks.

Above: The Barceloneta beach waterfront area. **Opposite:** A stretch of the Playa de la Barceloneta overlooking one of the wharfs at the Porto Olimpico.

TYLÖSAND
HALLAND

To the rest of the world, the name sounds more like an Ikea sofa than anything else, but to the Swedes Tylösand is the nation's top beach and summer just isn't summer without a trip down to Halland on the southwest coast. The soft light, the almost translucent colors of the sandy shore, and the scent of the low vegetation edging its soft sand are very North European indeed, but (surprise! surprise!) the water's not cold! Thanks to warm currents, it actually ranges between 64 and a balmy 71°F. It's also so clean that Tylösand was awarded a Blue Flag. But this place is also one of the most famous beaches—in fact, the English *Times* ranked it as one of the world's top 10 coolest beaches. In summer, this coastal town is invaded by young vacationers (up to 60,000 a day!) and comes alive with shows, concerts, sports competitions, exhibitions, and beach parties. Along its 4-mile length, you'll see joggers, windsurfers, kite surfers, sunbathers, and people just enjoying a drink in the bars. The weather is good, too, with an average of 71°F most days in summer.

The Tylösand Hotel is the real nerve center of the beach and it's from here that most of the action starts, both day and night. Music is the key. In the evenings Tylösand becomes one huge outdoor night club where everyone kicks off their shoes and dances the night away. The hotel is also a large contemporary art gallery featuring the work of mostly Scandinavian painters, sculptors, graphic artists, and photographers. The rich celebrity villa owners in the area tend to meet up in its bar. But if you like a more "natural" ambience, you might like to try First Camp Tylösand, a very good camping ground near the sea that's also child-friendly.

NEARBY

Tylösand is located about 5 miles outside the town of **Halmstad**. You can also drive to the beach, which lies between **Göteborg** and **Malmö**, from the city of Copenhagen in Denmark. The Tylösand area is also legendary for the fact that it has no less than 11 golf courses. The most famous of these is **Tylösands Golfklubb**, which is widely considered Sweden's finest and also one of the top 10 in Europe. If you are traveling with kids, try the nearby **Frösakull** beach or spend an afternoon checking out the rides at the **Äventyrs** adventure park. Both are great. Other beaches worth visiting in the vicinity are **Mellbystrand**, **Varberg**, and **Laholm**.

*Above: Tylösand is considered one of the top 10 most fun beaches in Europe. **Right**: Concerts, exhibitions, and shows that attract thousands of participants are all organized on Tylösand beach.*

HAT SAI KAEW
KOH SAMET

The Thais themselves will tell you that the beaches of Koh Samet are the whitest in the entire kingdom. This tiny island stretches 4 miles by 1 mile and is just a half-hour ferry ride from the east coast of Rayong. A former pirate haven, it was discovered in the 1970s by youngsters looking for a more peaceful existence far from the city chaos. Happily, this jealously guarded little corner of paradise has so far escaped the worst excesses of mass tourism and is turning into something of an exclusive destination, compared to Phuket and Koh Samui. Forget Ibiza, Negril, or Punta del Este, fun here is not about the jet set scene or easy sex. Edged by wild jungle on the Gulf of Thailand, the only place you'll find the *movida* in these parts is at Hat Sai Kaew or Diamond Beach in the northeast of the island. Spend your days here with a little sunbathing, some great massages, windsurfing, snorkeling, and diving. The partying starts as the sun goes down and the beer, local rum, or whisky begins to flow. At Bay Watch Bar, Silver Sand, Buddy, and Reggae bar, just enjoy the barbecues and spicy, coconut-perfumed Thai food from happy hour until late. It's a friendly, warm atmosphere, sometimes romantic, sometimes a little bizarre, too. Dig your toes into the sand as you recline on a silk cushion, listen to the music, smell the smoke, and watch fire-eaters and Thai kick boxers do their thing. There's also music on the beach or on little wooden stages.

The Royal Forest Department guards the island's natural heritage. Its marine ecosystem is still perfectly intact along the southern shore and around the uninhabited islets of Koh Khudi, Koh Thalu, and Koh Man Nai. The queen of Thailand ordered a turtle nursery to be founded there and the Samet archipelago was made a national park in 1981.

NEARBY

Relax in sophisticated private luxury at the **Paradee Resort**, a world apart on the southernmost tip of the island. It's nestled between two lovely beaches: one to the west with a sunset bar and the other, Ao Kiew, to the east with an infinity pool, restaurants, and 40 villas, some with their own private pools, cradling in the lush green vegetation. This is where the Thai Royal Family comes to vacation. Luxuriate in the treatments at the Spa and your private transfer by speedboat. The **Trat Islands**, farther south near Cambodia, also made the *New York Times*' list of 31 places to visit in 2010.

Above: The beach at Hat Sai Kaew, lively and atmospheric at sunset. **Right**: A view from above of a stretch of Hat Sai Kaew beach and its beautiful emerald waters.

JUMEIRAH BEACH UNITED ARAB EMIRATES
DUBAI

No palm trees here. Just a skyline of cement, stone, steel, and glass like no other: we're in Dubai, the buzzing financial heartland of the United Arab Emirates.

Jumeirah Beach extends from Jebel Ali Bay to Port Rashid and overlooks the world's most famous artificial islands. This is a place where every possible dream either has or soon will come true. And so after a bit of sunbathing and a swim in the warm, calm turquoise Persian Gulf, you might like to try a ride on a camel or perhaps one of the big wet bikes that zoom around The Crescent, one of the three palm-shaped artificial islands. Better still, go parasailing and enjoy the unique and slightly surreal sight of a city that has made breaking records its business. Dubai has the world's tallest skyscraper (Burj Khalifa), its only 7-star hotel (Burj Al Arab), the largest healthcare hub (Dubai Healthcare City: 90 clinics, 2 hospitals, 1,700 doctors, researchers, and nurses), the best-equipped indoor ski slope (Ski Dubai, 72,000 square feet), and even the largest amusement park (Dubailand, 107 square miles).

Up there, dangling from your parachute, you'll see the aforementioned 7-star hotel— a gigantic sail-like structure that was designed by WS Atkins and Partners dominating the horizon. There are huge buildings all around that look like fairy-tale castles, too. You'll even see a kind of Far Eastern version of the Venetian lagoon complete with fake gondolas and glittering canals. Last but very far from least is The World, an archipelago of 300 artificial islands in the shape of a world map. Also floating below are the magnificent villas of the rich and famous who have chosen Dubai as their home. The sights just go on and on: turn around and you'll face the Burj Khalifa, a skyscraper towering almost 2,717 feet. Officially the tallest building in the world, 10 floors of this magnificent building are used as a hotel by the legendary fashion designer Giorgio Armani.

NEARBY

Visit the old city—you'll save up to 30 percent on purchases in the **Gold Souk**—or a boat trip on **Dubai Creek**, a river/lagoon in the heart of the city. The latter has restaurants, stores, and even a water and theme park. Take a taxi boat (*abra*) from one side to the other. Try dinner or even tea at the **Burj Al Arab** (the only and rather expensive way of getting in to see the hotel interior), a dune safari, or even skiing at **Dubai Ski** in the Mall of Emirates. Finally, you should check out the **Hatta Heritage Village** (in the Shindagha area), which has reconstructed cane and mud houses, fortresses and lookout towers, and an artisan *souk*.

Opposite: Water slides in the amusement park on the waterfront at Jumeirah Beach. Left: The Burj El Arab, Dubai, the world's most luxurious hotel, which sits on an island linked to the beach by a suspended walkway.

When you finally get your feet back on the ground, or rather into the silky soft white sand, you'll probably just feel like going right back up again to feast your eyes on the sights. But instead why not make your way back along the beach and stretch out on your very luxurious sun lounger. You'll find that while you've been away, the hotel staff has brought out a selection of cooling wraps, a fresh beach towel, and a few tempting delicacies to nibble on. Once you've settled back into the shade, just allow your gaze to wander across this kitsch, sumptuous fantasy land: a place of contradictions that's both real and illusory.

Above: An atmospheric shot of camels on Jumeirah Beach. **Right:** *The Jumeirah Beach skyline seen from the sea off Dubai.*

BRIGHTON
EAST SUSSEX

Brighton is often said to have spawned modern seaside tourism. In 1750, medical doctor Richard Russell praised the benefits of sea bathing. Needless to say, the beau monde felt it its duty to try this particular cure and Brighton quickly became fashionable. Its fame burgeoned when the Prince of Wales, later George IV, built the Royal Pavilion, which remains one of Britain's most visited buildings. Brighton (now Brighton and Hove) has held its position as one of the coolest English cities as well as being hugely popular both with Her Majesty and more ordinary vacationers alike.

The sloping shore extends a full 7 miles from the suburb of Hove in the west to the modern Brighton Marina Village in the east. Two large constructions jut out into the sea: the West Pier, which was built in 1866 and destroyed by a storm in the 1970s, and the Palace Pier (better known as the Brighton Marine Palace and Pier), which has been going strong since 1899. The latter is a huge pleasure arcade jammed with old and modern amusements, games rooms, bars, restaurants, and stores. It also hosts a magnificent fireworks display every Saturday in August. There is a sandy section of the beach but you must pay to enter, and a charming string of colorful traditional English beach huts at Hove. Naturists have their own private area near Brighton Marina. Don't forget to explore the waterfront or, as it's known in these parts, the Esplanade: go on foot as this is the only way you'll get to do a bit of exploring and shopping in between stopping off in the many pubs, bars, tearooms, and restaurants lining it. Brighton is also set to become the first wireless beach.

NEARBY

The surrounding county of East Sussex is home to a wonderful collection of forests, castles, and cliffs. But don't forget to explore the streets of Brighton itself. Dip into the Steine and the **Lanes District**, a picturesque labyrinth lined with restaurants, pubs, fish and chip shops, boutiques, and much more. Take a trip down memory lane with a ride on **Volk's Electric Railway**. And no visit to Brighton would be complete without a stop at the **Royal Pavilion** and the adjacent **Brighton Museum & Art Gallery**. The nightlife is superb. Brighton also has a reputation as Britain's most gay, lesbian, and transgender-friendly town.

*Above: Brighton beach and the Esplanade are crowded at the height of the summer season. **Right:** The rocky shoreline and the legendary Brighton Marine Palace and Pier.*

CANNON BEACH
OREGON

United States Highway 101 unfolds along the Pacific coast of Oregon. Stunning vistas open up around every bend. The most breathtaking stretch of all, however, is between John Yeon State Park and Cape Kiwanda State Park.

To the south of the latter is the long expanse of Cannon Beach. Dominated by enormous black sea stacks offshore, this is a place that likes to keep its pleasure low key. It's the ideal spot, in fact, to spend hours strolling barefoot along the sand, watch blazing sunsets, enjoy romantic candlelit dinners in one of the many little coastal restaurants, and peruse the local art galleries. It's also great for watching the young surfers, who seem to be a natural part of the whole scenario, enjoying themselves on the waves.

Farther to the south, the landscape becomes even more spectacular and the atmosphere heats up. Just before sunset each evening, the beach at Cape Kiwanda fills up with pick-ups and off-roaders. Their sun-burnt occupants jump out and unload cases of beer, turn up their stereos, and then get down to some serious dancing, eating, and flirting. After sunset, amid much jubilant yelling and whistling, the beach party continues until everyone has had enough to drink and eat. Even during the day, the atmosphere is pretty lively at Cape Kiwanda. The beach is alive with volleyball games and there are always surfers out on the waves despite the chilly waters. This is a beach where people come to have fun and make plenty of noise. That said, though, there's even more to enjoy just around the next bend: lagoons, more beaches, and more rocky outcrops...

NEARBY

Don't miss the magnificent estuary of the Columbia River, just a little farther north of Cannon Beach. This is where the Lewis and Clark Expedition spent a very long, wet winter having finally made it to the ocean. It is also now home to a reconstructed version of the log fort they built for protection while they were there. All along the coast there are gorgeous towns like **Astoria** and **Warrenton**, once ordinary fishing villages and now tourist havens. Their wooden houses are protected as national monuments and the way of life in the area remains as simple, traditional, and bright as their delicate, pastel-colored facades.

Above: The mouth of the Columbia River is surrounded by an area of rare beauty. **Right**: The Cape Kiwanda sea stack. The beach directly in front of it fills up each evening at sunset with young partiers and their pick-ups.

They're tiny, evocative little corners of paradise and it's our duty to ensure they are protected for posterity. These are beaches where nature reigns supreme. Whether they are made of silky soft sand, tiny quartz crystals, crumbs of white coral, or sun- and sea-bleached pebbles, they are all lapped by dream-like seas. In some cases these beaches are also reserves for protected animals, sea turtles, or sea lions. They're special, endangered places, which we should approach not as vacationers but as "pilgrims of the Earth, respectful and careful at every step," as renowned Indian ecologist Vandana Shiva advises travelers in the third millennium.

Giuseppe Ortolano

PROTECTED
beaches

CALETA VALDÉS

CHUBUT

Protected just doesn't cover it. The impression you get in Caleta Valdés is that you really have stepped "out of this world." The peninsula from which the beach takes its name is a UNESCO World Heritage Site and as such is one of the world's most vast marine wildlife reserves. Located in the province of Chubut in northern Patagonia, Argentina, it has an ecosystem like no other area of the world. The plateau isn't any more than 300 feet above sea level, but it juts out into the Atlantic Ocean and is linked to the mainland by a 22-mile-long narrow strip of land known as the Amgeghino Isthmus. The peninsula's perimeter takes in over 250 miles of jagged coastline into which the tides have carved bays, inlets, islands, and two vast gulfs, San José to the north and Nuevo to the south, where the water temperature is less icy-cold than the ocean. It is along a stretch of the eastern coast that you will come upon the geographical oddity that is known to the world as Caleta Valdés, a sort of very long estuary that runs parallel to the sea. It is a 12-mile peninsula that has been eroded by the sea, forming tiny islands in the process (Primera, Segunda, Gaviota), which are visible or otherwise depending on the tides. Just inland from the coast, the sand dunes mask archaeological signs of the peninsula's original inhabitants, the Tehuelches Indians, who chose Caleta Valdés to collect shellfish and hunt guanacos. This place is a primordial landscape of endless horizons, windswept skies, and a coastline of fossilized shells washed up tens of millions of years ago. The sunsets are brilliantly clear and bright here because of the complete absence of any air or light pollution in this magnificent corner of the world. Animals reign supreme here: sea elephants, sea lions caring for their young, even a colony of Magellanic penguins, which have chosen this expanse of beach as their permanent home and don't seem in the least bit concerned by the arrival of awestruck humans, who've trekked across miles of prairie to see them.

NEARBY

The rocky, dusty *rutas de ripio* are dirt roads that run dead straight for mile after mile. Because they are so rough and rugged, you can only drive slowly along them, but the plus is that you can spend time admiring the prairie and animals. You'll meet groups of guanacos, odd-looking nandù with their strange gray plumage, rare armadillos, merino sheep, and tawny-tailed foxes. Take a trip to **Bird Island** near the Ameghino Isthmus to see millions of wonderful birds, while the old lighthouse on **Punta Delgada** is the place to watch sea elephants. Take a boat from the fishing village of **Puerto Pirámides**, the peninsula's only settlement, out into the calm waters of the bay to do a spot of **whale-watching**.

Opposite: The coast of the province of Chubut is the place to go for whale-watching. **Left**: Sea elephants and sea lions loll about happily on the beach at Caleta Valdés.

CAPE RANGE
WESTERN AUSTRALIA

To reach the west coast of Australia from most of the rest of the world entails traveling by plane for at least an entire day. Then you have to go another 740 miles if you want to get to the peninsula of Cape Range. It's about 60 miles in length, which is just a dot on the immense map of Australia. To give you an idea of the sizes we're talking about, we might mention that the State of Western Australia itself is about the size of Western Europe. It is also the wildest and least spoilt of the country's states, and the same can be said of its coastline. Most of the Cape Range peninsula's west coast, some 37 miles in length, belongs to the Cape Range National Park, where the outback gradually turns into beach. Slabs of granite that have been scratched by the wind for millions of years reach the sea, opening up onto cliff peaks and little fjords, colored by the famous Australian red earth and the green bushes of the hinterland.

The sand is totally white, thanks to the coral reef that protects it. Many people think that the Queensland coast is the home of Australia's only coral reef, but there's also one on the

NEARBY

Outside Cape Range National Park but still on the peninsula there are plenty of other beaches that are worth a visit: these include, most notably, **Town Beach**, the nearest to Exmouth, the region's capital; **Bundegi Beach**; and **Lighthouse Bay,** with the wreck of the SS **Mildura,** which has been half-submerged there since 1907. Also try **Coral Bay**, one of the towns along the 125 miles of Barrier Reef. It's a little south of the Cape Range peninsula just in front of the Ningaloo Marine Park, and has several beaches that deserve a visit. They include Bills Bay, the busiest, where the sand is silky soft and the water fantastic. You'll see young kids playing rugby on the shore and, well away from the umbrellas, cricket.

Above: A kangaroo rests in the luxuriant vegetation of Cape Range National Park.
Left: Amanta ray swims undisturbed in front of a deep sea diver. **Opposite**: *The clear water and unspoilt beaches of Cape Range.*

other side of the continent. The Ningaloo Reef (which forms part of a marine park of the same name) is every bit as fascinating, containing countless species of colorful tropical fish, 180 types of coral, and thousands of whale sharks, gentle giants that are more than 30 feet in length and over 11 tons in weight. They migrate here and stay from the middle of March to the middle of May. They love to cavort between the boats of those brave enough to approach them. Whale-watching is one of the favorite tourist pastimes around these parts. Heading out from the shore in a boat can provide a unique experience, in addition to allowing you the chance to admire the coastline in all its glory. South of Tantabiddi, not far from Coral Bay, you can find ecolodges on the beach. They offer the best way to enjoy the coast. They are highly exclusive places, but at the same time they enable you to stay in close contact with nature and the sea. Hidden among the dunes in the area's more unspoilt corners, you'll find a series of enormous tents that are outfitted with every possible comfort. Here you can witness spectacular sunrises and sunsets and enjoy the feeling of being in a perfect world. Many young surfers sleep in small tents inside the park in order to experience the same sensations, but at the risk of heavy fines.

The semi-permanent lodges are also the starting point for trekking itineraries to the far corners of an area where the flora and fauna exists far from any human influence.

Some stretches of the coastline are completely uninhabited and difficult to reach; in fact you might not see another human being for weeks. Other beaches are largely deserted and can be approached easily by kayak or on foot. Of the 43 miles of coast, only a few hundred yards are considered organized beaches and they tend to be close to the lodges. Here the favorite pastime is snorkeling, especially on the south side of the park, where the coral reef is richer. Rugby, soccer, beach volleyball, and cricket are the more popular beach sports here. Most of the tourists are local families or people from Perth, as there are very few foreigners who vacation here. It's a place that you come across almost by chance, but you'll never want to leave.

Opposite: *Peak formations of red rock on the sea at Cape Range.* **Above:** *An ecolodge at the edge of the beach.* **Right:** *The beach at Cape Range.*

SHROUD CAY
EXUMA

One of the most fascinating sights seen by astronauts orbiting Earth is the color of the waters around Exuma, a group of small islands in the Bahamas. Its 365 islands unfold like a string of pearls and are surrounded by sheltered bays and large coral reefs. The ones with the best facilities are Great Exuma, Little Exuma, and Staniel Cay, which was used by the director Terence Young to shoot some of the finest scenes in the legendary James Bond movie *Thunderball* (1965). It's difficult to actually pinpoint any beach in particular as hardly any have official names.

The islands are all incredibly beautiful, with coral sandy beaches surrounded by spectacular seas and sandy seabeds rich in colorful flora and fauna. Shroud Cay has all of these and a pinch of extra magic besides that makes it just that bit more spectacular than its sisters. If you dive, you'll get to explore the so-called blue holes, which include the Hurricane Hole, a protected grotto near Elizabeth Harbor beach. Then there's Mystery Cave, near the semi-deserted Stocking Island. Snorkeling fans will be able to get to Thunderball Grotto, which teems with tropical fish, while thrill-seekers can look forward to close encounters with sharks at Amberjack Reef. Exuma also hosts plenty of fishing competitions throughout the year, including the Annual Bonefish Tournament, a major event which takes place in July at the Staniel Cay Yacht Club and which attracts entrants from all over the globe. The archipelago is also home to the Exuma Cays Land and Sea Park, which was set up in 1958 and encompasses around a dozen islands. The capital of the Exumas is George Town, and this is where most of the tourist accommodation and facilities are located, with everything available from the major hotel chains to small resorts nestling in tranquil tropical gardens.

NEARBY

You can't leave without a boat trip to one of the island's many deserted coves (there are over 265). The most characteristic is **Allan's Cay Iguanas**, the habitat of the rare Bahaman iguana. **Thunderball Grotto**, **Hurricane Hole**, and **Exuma Land and Sea Park** are all musts for snorkeling fans. Exuma's history is laid bare at **Hermitage Plantation House**, the vestiges of one of the earliest plantations built around 1783. The **Exuma Family Island Regatta** is one of the oldest events in the Bahamas and attracts 50 or so hand-built boats, which sail into George Town from all over the archipelago.

*Above: The little islands making up the Exuma archipelago can only be reached by boat or sea plane. **Right**: Seen from above, Shroud Cay and the surrounding islands are almost surreally beautiful.*

PRAIA DO FORTE

BAHIA

P raia do Forte is at the very start of the Linha Verde, the national highway that runs north along the Brazilian coast to Jandaira. It is 52 miles from the capital city of the state of Bahia, Salvador, where the locals have managed to strike just the right balance between tourism and keeping the area intact. This is the municipality of Mata de São João, otherwise known as Brazil's Polynesia. Praia do Forte is a fishing village, which was a private *fazenda* (estate) until the 1970s. Its beach extends for a breathtaking 25 miles along the coast, taking in dunes, palms, marshland, rivers, and fishing villages. Praia do Forte is Brazil's third oldest town. The main drag, Alameda do Sol, is lined by lively local restaurants and bars and leads to a waterfront square on which the Capela de São Francisco de Assis and the sea turtle reserve are located. The beach is a huge expanse of silky soft white sand that dazzles against the deep blue sea. Its only inhabitants are some incredibly willowy coconut trees. Along it, there are lovely natural pools where you can snorkel (the Lord and Papa Gente being two examples).

The rest of the blue lagoon is ideal for rowing and has a nice breeze to keep you cool. There are also private beaches with sun loungers and umbrellas and palms providing just the right amount of shade from the hot sun. The best time to be here is between March and October, but even during the rest of the year, it's hot and there's very little rain. The Praia do Forte eco-reserve covers 7.5 miles of sandy coastline. Common, green, bastard, and Hawksbill turtles are all monitored and protected under the highly successful Tamar Project. Researchers also study the animals' egg-laying season between September and March. There are more than 500 nests along the 30 miles of coastline under observation, and fishermen help in this process. The project encompasses 18 stations spread over 60 miles of coastline to the north, but the operational base is at Praia do Forte. Don't miss a boat trip to whale-watch offshore.

NEARBY

Everywhere in the village you'll see people doing the *roda de capoeira*, a Brazilian specialty that is half-dance, half-marital art. You'll also see Candomblè ceremonies (part of the Afro-Brazilian religion). Inland from Praia do Forte is the **Reserva da Sapiranga**: 1,480 acres that are home to various native species of plants and flowers. You can do various activities here including hiking, cycling, and zip-lining (shooting across rivers on a rope). Do visit the ruins of the **Castelo do Garcia d'Ávila**, the earliest significant Portuguese building in Brazil. It goes all the way to the border with the state of Maranhão. There are organized tours from the village to **Salvador** as well as visits to the **Morro de São Paulo, Itacaré**, and **Ilhéus**.

*Above: Some monkeys belonging to the Callitrichid family hiding in the dense vegetation at Praia do Forte. **Opposite:** The sandy, rocky beach at Praia do Forte, a vast protected area running along the coast of Salvador.*

BAHÍA GARDNER
GALÁPAGOS

To land at Bahía Gardner, one of the most beautiful beaches in the entire Galápagos Islands, you'll quite literally have to take the plunge. There are no docks here, no jetties, no roads. The only way to visit this little corner of paradise is by boat. You'll cast off from Puerto Ayora on the island of Santa Cruz, the archipelago's main tourist hub, and then make your way south-west for a good 10 to 12 hours. Then almost by magic, Española, the oldest and southernmost of what seafarers call the Enchanted Islands, appears over the horizon. Once you sail into the bay that hugs the white sand and coral beach, you'll probably find yourself surrounded by playful sea lions, who tend to welcome visitors with twirls and pirouettes. There are no facilities on the island whatsoever as it is uninhabited, so you'll just have to jump out of your boat and into the water. Española is part of the Galápagos National Park and it's well worth getting wet to go here and pick your way along a beach crowded with sea lions and birds of various kinds. Then get back into the water for some snorkeling or go to nearby Gardner Island. Between October and December, the stretch of sea off the beach is the playground of young turtles of the Chelonia. Mydas variety, also known as Pacific Green Sea Turtles. The island is an absolute gem and is home to around 10,000 pairs of albatross, which are considered the world's most spectacular sea birds. There are also masked and blue-footed boobies, pelicans, Darwin finches, all sorts of gulls, buzzards, and other birds. At nearby Punta Suarez, you'll be able to stroll around through marine iguanas and lava lizards as you admire the stunning 60-foot-high jet of sea water shooting out through a sort of marine geyser created by a small crack in the rock.

NEARBY

The closest island to Española is the lovely and gentle **Floreana**, a place so sweet that even the cacti don't have any thorns! Around 50 people live on the island and the hotel there is run by a family whose forbears arrived in the Galápagos in the early 20th century in search of the last remaining "paradise lost." In **Bahía del Correo**, you can still see the barrel, which sailors from around 1783 onward used to fill with letters home, knowing that passing ships would pick them up and send them on.

*Above: Some visitors enjoy a bit of snorkeling with the local sea lions. **Right**: The dazzlingly white beach at Bahía Gardner, which is home to sea lions who basically ignore human company.*

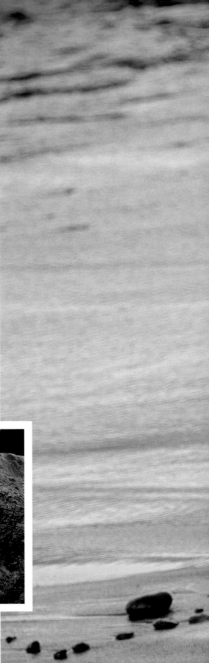

RABIDA
GALÁPAGOS

The intensity of the colors will quite literally take your breath away. The lace-like emerald green vegetation edging the shore at Rabida Beach on the island of the same name is a feast for the eyes. The dark red of the shore itself contrasts beautifully with the periwinkle blue of the sea and the gray of the lava flows. Like all of the other islands in the Galápagos chain, the 2.5 square miles of Rabida is, of course, volcanic. Rabida, also known as Jervis, has its own rules. The first one is a wet landing for all visitors, but it's only a few steps through the sea to the beach. The guide accompanying you will enforce plenty more, too: you have to stay at least 13 feet from all animals at all times. You can't touch or take away anything. This is, after all, an island described by UNESCO as "a living museum and evolutionary showcase." On the vermillion red beach, which owes its color to iron deposits, you'll find yourself flanked by sea lions dipping in and out of the sea or lolling casually in the sun, completely unfazed by human contact. Not far away, around a saltwater lagoon, you'll see some adolescent males waiting for the dominant male to allow them to approach the colony. The rocks along the beach are great for snorkeling, and you'll have giant mantas, marine iguanas, sea turtles, and hammerhead sharks for company. Glass-bottomed boats allow the less adventurous to admire the dazzlingly colorful marine life and underwater world. If you leave the beach and walk up a path between *palo santo* (holy stick) trees (used to make incense) and opuntia cactus, you'll come upon colonies of pelicans and blue-footed boobies who nest on the reddish ground here. At sunset, Rabida Beach turns gold and russet as flocks of curlews with long red beaks forage along the shore for their dinner.

NEARBY

One of the islands near Rabida is **Santa Cruz**, the most densely populated of the 18 making up the archipelago. Not far from Puerto Ayora, the main town, is the **Charles Darwin Research Center**, where there is a special nursery for endangered giant turtles that are then returned to their natural habitat. There are two airports, one on the island of Baltra and the other at Puerto Baquerizo Moreno, the capital of the Galápagos, on San Cristóbal. The best way to get around the islands is by boat, but you can also stay on one of the larger islands and then take trips out to the others each day.

Above: Red crabs scrabbling across the rocks on Rabida Beach. Right: A young male sea lion shows off on the sand at Rabida, which is an unusual vermillion red.

CAP DE LA HAGUE
NORMANDY

A peninsula within a peninsula: Cap de la Hague is the western-most point of Cotentin, the area of Normandy that stretches out into the sea towards the south coast of England. There's an end-of-the-world atmosphere there (*bout du monde* as the French call it). You may not be quite at the end of the world, but you are at the end of mainland Europe. The landscape here is almost Irish with Atlantic moorland, blazing red with heather, running right up the edge of dizzyingly high cliffs that plunge into the ocean beneath. Protected by the Conservatoire du Littoral, these are the landscapes you'll see in the paintings of Jean-François Millet. Jacques Prévert loved the area and actually spent the last part of his life in the village of Omonville-la-Petite. The jewel in this rough-hewn crown of a place is Ecalgrain Bay, which has a wonderfully isolated sandy beach. The coast is jagged in these parts, reaching heights of almost 400 feet in places. But even from the cliff tops you can still hear the Atlantic beating away at the rock beneath. Out in the bay is the island of Alderney. Between you and it is the Raz Blanchard, one of the most perilous stretches of sea in the world. When the tides are high, currents can reach speeds of 18 knots (around 20 miles per hour). Ironically, this is also one of the busiest sea channels in the world, traversed by more than 600 ships a day. They are guided to safety by the La Hague Light, built in 1826. Towering 150 feet into the windswept sky, it is a welcome beacon to anyone who has to negotiate the Raz Blanchard. The best way to explore Ecalgrain Bay is to take the Gr 223 footpath, which is known locally as the customs officers' path, towards Nez de Voidries and Nez de Jobourg. It is advisable to keep to the signposted paths because this is a lonely, treacherous place in which high cliffs, winds, and fog can catch you unawares. The flora and fauna is wild. You'll see lots of sea birds including the solan goose (northern gannet) and tufted cormorant. Farther south, the path runs down from the cliffs to a huge sandy beach edged by sand dunes in Vauville Bay, which extends for 5 miles to Cap de Flamanville.

NEARBY

Coutances Cathedral has to be one of Cotentin's and Normandy's most stunning gothic treasures and has rather unfairly been somewhat overshadowed by nearby Mont Saint-Michel. Gargoyles, towers, and stained-glass windows adorn what was originally a Romanesque structure completed in 1056 for the children of Tancred of Hauteville. They set off from the town to conquer southern Italy and went on to play a determining role in the history of both Sicily and Puglia. At the time, Coutances was the largest city in Cotentin, and it is now a dynamic little town that was rebuilt around its cathedral after it was destroyed in the bombings of June 6, 1944.

*Above: A picturesque view of the landscape near Cap de la Hague. **Opposite:** The beach and cliffs at Ecalgrain Bay at Cap de la Hague.*

LA DOUBLE
CAVALLO ISLAND

The island of Cavallo was a favorite of the ancient Romans and many reminders of their presence survive to this day. The Romans quarried precious granite here, which along with granite from Capo Testa in Sardinia, was transported back to the mainland. La Double beach was one of the locations quarried. Its name comes from the fact that it overlooks the sea on two fronts: one or other of its sides is therefore usually sheltered from the wind, which can be very strong indeed. Cavallo is located in French waters in the Bouches de Bonifacio straits. It is the loveliest island in the Lavezzi archipelago, offering 10 miles of beaches and coves hidden away amongst the rocks. It is also halfway between Corsica and Sardinia. It is private and its vegetation is still completely unspoilt despite the presence of a luxury hotel and various villas owned by the rich and famous. Or perhaps the very fact that it is so private and exclusive has actually helped preserve its very special beauty by holding at bay any massive developments or tourist influx. Its sea is turquoise and its beaches a lovely white and pink because of the tiny shells known as Saint Lucy's Eyes and fragments of red coral. Myrtle and juniper bushes spring up between the rocks, which the wind and waves have sculpted into the oddest of shapes. The result is an almost surreal scenario. The best months to visit the island, its sea, and beaches are June and September. If you move inland a bit you'll find footpaths and a few dirt roads that you'll only be able to traverse on foot, by bicycle, or electric car. Until a very short time ago, in fact, it wasn't even possible to disembark on the island or anchor in the vicinity. Now, however, there's a small, well-equipped port. The Lavezzi Islands, which include Cavallo, Piana, and Ratino, are treacherous indeed, with rocks lying in wait just beneath the surface of the shallow waters. You will need to keep a nautical chart and official pilot's book at hand at all times.

NEARBY

There are many hidden treasures around La Double beach, including the island's other gorgeous beaches. Granite **Lavezzi** is home to a small cemetery in which are interred the remains of the victims of the shipwreck of the **Sémillante**, a French frigate that went down on the rocks here in 1855. Then there is the tiny **Piana**, an island you can walk to across a very shallow stretch of water at Piantarella on the Corsican coast. The Lavezzi Islands are also within easy reach of **La Maddalena** and its islands: Caprera, **Razzoli**, **Budelli**, and many more. You can get the ferry from nearby **Bonifacio**, and be in **Santa Teresa di Gallura** within 20 minutes. If you decide to take the ferry, you can't leave without a trip to **Capo Testa**.

Above: The rocks on the island of Cavallo take on a truly magical glow at sunset.
Opposite: The beautifully sheltered La Double Bay.

ACCIAROLI

CAMPANIA

Silky, golden sand, a climate that's warm even when summer is still a far-off dream. The beach at Acciaroli is a truly wonderful discovery on a fine spring day. The coast slopes away gently into the sea and, despite the fact that the water is so shallow, it is still wonderful, clean, and clear. The beach itself is tufted with the rare sea lily, a protected species that grows naturally on certain bits of the Italian coastline and fills the air with a deliciously heady perfume. The municipality belongs to the Cilento and Vallo di Diano National Park, 447,189 acres spread across the province of Salerno and recognized by UNESCO as a Biosphere Reserve in 1998. This is a habitat that's home to olive trees hundreds of years old. It's also a place whose human inhabitants live exceptionally long and healthy lives, thanks to their surroundings and (as was proven by research into the famous Mediterranean diet, begun in the area in 1951 by a Minnesota professor Ancel Keys) the food they eat. Keys actually moved to Acciaroli with his wife, and lived to be 100 (1904–2004). A few days' vacation here is enough to revive even the most exhausted of spirits. The same visitors return year after year to their usual hotels overlooking the sea, or rent apartments in the lush hills. Children play freely and nature enthusiasts have a field day spotting marine flora and fauna. Lazier vacationers simply relax in the sun until evening when they watch the sun slide beneath the horizon like a fiery red ball. It is said that Ernest Hemmingway spent quite some time in the fishing village of Acciaroli in the 1950s. Whether this is true or not, what is indeed certain is that his character from *The Old Man and the Sea* would have looked right at home amid the wooden boats in this tourist port.

NEARBY

To the south, there is **Ascea**, which the Romans called "Velia and the Greeks Elsea." This was where Parmenides founded his school of philosophy in the 5th century BC, of which Zeno was a member. This archaeologically rich area includes the **Porta Rosa** (Rosa's Gate), a rare example of a 4th-century BC Greek round arch in Italy. It's perfectly preserved because it lay buried under a mound of earth for centuries before being discovered in 1964 by the archaeologist Mario Napoli, who dedicated it to his wife Rosa. Moving on you'll get to **Capo Palinuro**. Charter a boat to explore the sea caves along the coast, like the Blue Grotto.

*Above: A spectacular sunset over the sea at Acciaroli. **Right:** The clear blue sea at the beach at Acciaroli in springtime.*

IERANTO
CAMPANIA

It was Strabo, the legendary 1st-century BC Greek geographer, who first suggested that the Li Galli islands were once the home of sirens. In Greek mythology only Odysseus and Jason managed to resist the charms of Parthenope, Leucosia, and Ligeia, who lived off the Bay of Ieranto. Even the briefest visit to this area gives a good idea why. The Bay of Ieranto is the largest and deepest on the Sorrento peninsula. It is also wonderfully intact and offers one of the most beautiful walks in the entire area. It opens up immediately south of Punta della Campanella and the 2 miles of coastline it occupies include two beaches which directly overlook Capri. Ieranto Grande, a pebble beach, is inaccessible over land and has steep limestone cliffs behind it. A small bluff separates it from what's known as Ieranto Piccola (Little Ieranto) or Marinella beach. This is a compact inlet with a sandy, pebbly beach from which you can see the Tower of Minerva to the northeast and farther out the Capri sea stacks. Ieranto beach was made part of the Punta della Campanella Protected Marine Area in 2002, and can be reached by a 1 mile footpath that runs through the low Mediterranean shrub. The first stretch is mainly holly oak and carob. Farther on, however, after the Villa Rosa, overlooking the village of Marina del Cantone (where Norman Douglas wrote *Siren Land*), euphorbia, mastic, myrtle, and juniper all flourish. But there's more to this area than nature, there are also areas of archaeological interest. From Ieranto beach itself you can see what remains of a mining village dating back to the early 20th century. There was a working limestone quarry on the promontory that stretches from Montalto Tower to the sea, and it supplied the Ilva blast furnaces at Bagnoli until 1945. It was closed down and abandoned, and then in 1986 was donated by Italsider to Fai (the Italian Foundation for the Environment), which restored the mine buildings and olive groves, a total of 117 acres, to their former glory.

NEARBY

To get to Ieranto Bay (Via Ieranto) start your journey from **Via Amerigo Vespucci**, just after Piazzetta di Nerano in the district of Massa Lubrense. The same square is home to the little church of **San Salvatore,** which has a nave and three side aisles and dates back to the first half of the 15th century. About 1 mile along the road, which is absolutely stunning but tortuous, you will get to the seafaring village of **Marina del Cantone**. From there take a path and you'll come to a 16th-century coastguard tower. About 15 minutes later you'll get to **Recommone beach**. A branch off the path to the Bay of Ieranto will bring you to the chapel of **Monte San Costanzo** (1,555 ft.).

Opposite: The little beach at Ieranto, a genuine treasure sheltered by the Sorrento peninsula. **Left:** *The tip of Punta della Campanella, south of which is the Bay of Ieranto.*

IS ARUTAS
SARDINIA

Simply going on the sound of it, Is Arutas would seem to be a name derived from the Italian for "ruins," "rocks," or "caves." But it's tricky enough tracing etymology in an area in which no less than three dialects are spoken: Campidanese, Catalan, and Logudorese. We are, of course, in Sinis on Sardinia's less well-known and wilder western coast. The Sinis Peninsula—Mal di Ventre Island Protected Marine Area was set up by ministerial decree in 1907, and the Is Arutas beach, which overlooks that area, is itself protected by municipal law. The colors here are intense, and there's a stunning contrast between the dazzling white of the shore and the blue of the sea. It's only when you actually get down to the beach that you realize how unusual it is: it's neither sand nor shingle but consists of millions of grains of quartz. Erosion begun thousands of years ago has resulted in this incredible rarity. Each pink, green, and white granule has been worn smooth to the size of a grain of rice as a result of the crumbling away of the granite base jutting out from under the island of Mal di Ventre. Those eroded rocks no longer exist, and the fossil beach of Is Arutas needs to be preserved to prevent it from disappearing. After decades of vandalism by individuals who simply took away tons of sand to decorate their homes, the beach had halved in size and the Mayor of Cabras issued an ordinance whose provisions included the fact that anyone on the beach has to wear closed shoes so as not to take a single grain with them when they leave. The strings of seaweed strewn along the shore are posidonia from the sea floor—it, too, is protected. This is like an al fresco spa, as even stretching out on this primordial beach where it's hard to get as much as a cell phone signal is a truly reinvigorating experience.

NEARBY

This is a great place to visit the prehistoric *nuraghi*. Go to **Tharros**, which is at the very end of the Sinis Peninsula. This was a Phoenician trading post in the 8th century BC and an important Carthaginian naval base in the 6th century BC before being taken over by the Romans in 238 BC until the 11th century AD, when it was abandoned by its citizens, who founded Ortisano instead. Now partly submerged in the sea, all that remains of the city today are the Roman and early Christian ruins. On the ancient Roman roads you'll see more ruins of buildings, thermal baths, the foundations of a temple, an amphitheater, and the *castellum aquae*, the town's main water reservoir.

*Above: The crystal clear waters of the sea near the beach at Is Arutas. **Right**: The contrast between the white of the quartz beach and the turquoise of the sea at Is Arutus is absolutely stunning.*

TORRE SALSA
SICILY

A solitary beach with magical views of chalky cliffs, limestone rock formations, and crystal clear water. That's Torre Salsa, which lies between Agrigento and Sciacca on the Sicilian coast. It is one of the most beautiful of Sicily's many beaches and a World Wildlife Fund (WWF) reserve established in 2000. Open year-round, the beach has four different entry points near Montallegro. Nudism is practiced here, too. Long sandy stretches alternate with rockier areas, making it the perfect habitat for a host of protected species, including the peregrine falcon and the endangered *Caretta caretta* or loggerhead sea turtle, which nests between the rocks. There are guided visits to these areas organized by WWF that are ideal for families and school children alike. The 1,877-acre area is gently terraced and is home to marshland that dries out in summer. It encompasses a variety of ecosystems ranging from Mediterranean maquis to wetlands and sand dunes. The underlying limestone marl is covered by layers of clay. The gorgeous beach is accessible only by narrow pathways through the rocks. The sea is crystalline and the whole area lush with euphorbia, mastic, and grass. There are also rare flowers abounding. Needless to say, dozens of species of birds make the area their home, from buzzards to egrets, gulls, and crows. The North African *Danaus chrysippus* butterfly has also been spotted here. There are stunning views along "Juniper Valley," with stretches of blue clay along the shore, limestone marl eroded by the wind, and the explosion of colors and perfumes from the Mediterranean thistle, orchids, anemones, and irises. As you walk towards the lovely ruins of Eraclea Minoa, you'll also come upon the ancient watchtower that gives the entire reserve its name.

NEARBY

Not too far from the Valley of the Temples in Agrigento, Torre Salsa beach falls within the municipal area of **Siculiana Marina**, a small fishing town with an old castle. On the stretch of coastline up as far as Sciacca, you'll see **The Turkish Staircase**, near Realmonte. Over the centuries the wind has sculpted the white cliffs into a kind of natural staircase that juts out to the sea. Not far away is the archaeological site of **Eraclea Minoa**, an ancient Greek town. Don't miss **Porto Empedocle** and the stunning natural phenomenon that is **Vulcanetti di Maccalube**, volcano cones that ooze methane gas and salty mud.

*Above: The yellow limestone marl cliffs at Torre Salsa teeter over the beach. **Right:** A stretch of beach at Torre Salsa is still completely unspoilt even in the 21st century.*

PLAYA BLANCA
HOLBOX

Blissfully unravaged by mass tourism, Holbox is an island on the northern tip of the Yucatan, a place that has become a byword for unspoilt beauty. It is a place of pilgrimage for divers, who come here in search of whale sharks, majestic animals as difficult to spot as they are magnificent. Holbox, however, is the one place on earth you will likely see them. And within this earthly paradise is another, even more other-worldly spot: the Playa Blanca, a dazzlingly white and completely deserted beach. If you cast off from this idyllic location in one of the small, fast local boats, you'll easily get to an area of shallows in the Gulf of Mexico where the whale sharks congregate each year in families, between May and September. You can't get near to them in the boats, but amazingly you can swim with these gentle giants of the sea quite safely. And all under the watchful eye of the nature wardens: it is expressly forbidden to touch the sharks or for more than one person to be in the water with them at any time. You'll also see manta rays, dolphins, and hawksbill sea turtles. The experience is so magical that you'll find yourself wondering if you dreamt it all when you're back ashore. Holbox Island is a strip of sand populated by thousands of sea birds and its waters teem with fish and also the plankton on which the mild-mannered whale sharks feed. Despite their enormous size (up to 38 feet in length), the sharks are completely harmless. There are no black-top roads on the island and you'll be able to stroll barefoot on the sandy streets of the little local town, which has small restaurants and a few shops. You can rent golf carts, kayaks, or motorboats if you want to get around slightly faster. The only hotels are along the beach, and there's something for all tastes and pockets. There are scheduled ferries from Chiquilà to Holbox Island or you can get there by bus or car from Cancún.

NEARBY

Very few people know about it but the 1,000-year-old tree just outside **Chiquilà** is worth a visit. In the same area, there are three great destinations that will prove that the Yucatan isn't just all about all-inclusive resorts and theme parks. The first is the **Rio Lagartos Biosphere Reserve**, whose pristine beaches are home to thousands of pink flamingos. You can also take eco-tours of the forests to try to spot spider monkeys. The best of these are to be found at **Punta Laguna** and **Rancho Chablè**. Last but not least, you have to visit the Mayan city of **Ek Balam**, with its astonishingly well-preserved frescoed walls.

Above: The tiny island of Holbox has white sandy beaches and a warm welcome for visitors. *Right:* The Playa Blanca is a deliciously deserted beach, a pristine corner of the word jealously guarded by proud locals.

GOLDEN BEACH
NANGOMI

A paradise for sea turtles (*Caretta caretta*), which nest here, Cyprus's Golden Beach is actually one of the most widely admired nature reserves in the Mediterranean. Protected to the north by the Karpas National Park, home to wild donkeys, and to the east by the Apostolos Andreas monastery, this long sandy beach stretches almost 3 miles along Nangomi Bay in the northern part of the island, which has been controlled by Turkey since 1974, and is now part of the Turkish Republic of Northern Cyprus (a state not recognized by the Un). This is the district of di Famagosta and is practically deserted. The road taking you here isn't hard-topped and the beach is quite empty even at the height of summer. A few small *tavernas* offer simple food and drink and rent out sun loungers and umbrellas. The choice of accommodation is limited, with only a few small hotels around, but you are guaranteed absolute peace and quiet. There is a lively breeze on Golden Beach that makes the 95°F heat of summer a lot more bearable. The scene is seductive indeed. Just behind you are dunes and hills tufted with brush vegetation and out in front of you is a crystal clear sea that's perfect for sailing, windsurfing, diving, and swimming. The warmth of the water in this part of the Mediterranean is what sets it apart—temperatures never go below 70°F in April and May and rise to 77–79°F in full summer. Just nearby is the town of Famagosta, which in Greek means "hidden in the sand." It is famous for the long siege that took place there in 1571 that ended in the Turks expelling the Venetians. The latter may have lost the battle but their steadfast defense proved a determining factor in the organization of the Battle of Lepanto, in which the Ottoman fleet was completely wiped out by the Holy League.

NEARBY

Right near the Golden Beach is the **Apostolos Andreas Monastery** perched above the sea. Don't miss a visit as legend has it that the apostle stopped here en route to Palestine and caused a miraculous spring to appear. Another good trip is to the lively seaside city of **Famagosta**, the largest town in Northern Cyprus. There are some fine examples of medieval architecture in the old town center: Famagosta's fortifications are amongst the most important in the Mediterranean, and the city was always one of the key ports on the route from Europe to the Middle East.

*Above: The hills on Cyprus's northern coast are tufted with brushy vegetation. **Right:** Golden Beach and its extraordinary gold-tinted sand.*

ANSE LATIO
PRASLIN

NEARBY

Take a trip to **La Digue**, a real gem of an island just off the coast of Praslin and almost directly opposite Anse Latio. It's renowned as one of the most beautiful of the Seychelles thanks to its cooling palm trees, tiny beaches, imposing granite boulders, and turquoise waters. The fish market at **La Passe** is a wonderfully lively experience and the main mode of transport is ox and cart! Once you've disembarked the ferry from Prasin Island, take a bicycle trip up to the plateau, which extends from Grand Anse all the way to Anse Fourmis. **Anse Source d'Argent** is dazzling and you get there by crossing through an estate that's home to a family of giant land tortoises. As its name suggests, this is a white sandy beach with a silvery sheen.

Heaven on earth, there's no other way to describe it: a sheltered bay flanked by massive granite boulders shaped and smoothed by the elements over thousands if not millions of years. They sit there at either end of the beach like huge sculptures put there specifically to complement the crescent of crystalline water. Anse Latio beach on the island of Praslin in the Seychelles lies about 7 miles from Baie Sainte Anne. This is a stunningly beautiful place with incredibly silky sand, clear turquoise waters, those huge weather pink granite boulders, and a fringe of shady cocotiers (coconut trees). Praslin is also home to some of the oldest and tallest palm trees in the world in its Vallée de Mai—800-year-old specimens that tower 130 feet into the air. The female fruit of the latter, known as *cocos de mer*, are the largest in the world and the symbol of the Seychelles themselves. It is said that these outsized seeds, which are the same shape as a woman's pelvis, originally came from the deep and have supernatural powers. Anse Latio is ranked as one of the top 10 beaches in the world, and deservedly so. Film director Roman Polanski shot some of the finest scenes from his movie *Pirates*, starring Walter Matthau, here. When you leave the boat dock at Baie Sainte Anne, turn left and then head north to get to Anse Latio. Alternatively you can take the bus for Mont Plasir and get off at the last stop (a very steep 5-minute run) and then hike for a half hour or so through the spectacular lush countryside. You'll suddenly find yourself looking down at Anse Latio, floating there below you like a gorgeous, sun-kissed mirage. The best time to go is in the morning because in the afternoon the high tide covers the entire beach. The beach's crystalline waters offer superb snorkeling. In between swims you can sample the fish and seafood at two restaurants nearby: Le Chevalier and Bonbon Plume. The latter offers wonderful views of the beach and has both an inside dining room and a few tables set out on the sand itself. Unforgettable!

*Above: The slender strip of sand that is Anse Latio. **Opposite:** The spectacular rock formations at Anse Source d'Argent on La Digue, just opposite Anse Latio.*

GOUKAMMA
WESTERN CAPE

The Boers must have had a soft spot for this nature reserve because it was so similar to their homeland of Holland. There's something about the expanse of dunes licked into shape by the ocean winds, the choreographic display of bushy vegetation, and the sand that is almost eerily reminiscent of the beaches of the North Sea. The only thing is that the coast of the Netherlands doesn't have the one feature that makes this beach in the Goukamma Nature Reserve and Protected Area unique: the red sandstone rocks that line the shore. Just where sand and water meet, you'll see their jagged tops jutting out of the beach here and there. The rocks really do add a sense of movement, life, and color to the dazzling backdrop. Their pleasantly bizarre shapes fire the imagination: some look like dragons breathing fire into the air while others are like stylized giraffes whose necks are stretching skyward. It's lovely to stop here at sunset, feast your eyes on the array of shapes and sizes, and let your mind wander. The only sound will be the ebb and flow of the tide and the strident cries of the gulls. Otherwise,

NEARBY

Most of the tourist activity in the area focuses around **Knysna**, particularly in summer (December to February). At one end of the town is a peaceful lagoon surrounded by spectacular forest and, in fact, the area is famous for its wood-working. The lagoon is flanked by a golf course, which has absolutely super views. Knysna hosts a very well-known arts festival each September and also the Pink Loerie Festival in May. Oysters are now being farmed in the lagoon. Don't miss a visit to **Plettenberg Bay**, where there's the world's largest free-flight aviary. Plettenberg is also home to Monkeyland, where the monkeys are all free-roaming and protected.

*Above: This gorgeous bird is just one of the many colorful inhabitants of the Goukamma Nature Reserve. **Left**: A view of Buffalo Bay and the sensitive development along its shores. **Opposite**: Goukamma's long beach.*

silence reigns. Goukamma lies well beyond the thronged seafront at Knysna, one of the region's busiest coastal resorts. We are in South Africa, on the Western Cape, to be precise.

This is the Garden Route, almost 300 miles from Cape Town and 180 from Port Elizabeth. The Goukamma Nature Reserve extends outwards for a good 12 miles from Buffalo Bay, and the same again from the tourist hub of Knysna. It includes a big freshwater lake populated by more than 100 species of birds, including the rare Knysna toucan. The reserve is also home to a herd of rather adventurous antelope who like to flirt outrageously with the tourists. The beach is perfect for families but doesn't have any real tourist facilities whatsoever because it is part of the reserve, so you will have to come well prepared for all eventualities if you are bringing kids with you. Nonetheless, there is a very friendly campsite that you can stay in. If you like cycling, you'll love the wonderful bike trail that runs around the beach. You can pedal along the shore so close to the water you'll feel the spray from the waves breaking on the rocks, on your face. No cars are allowed on the reserve, so from the bridge over Goukamma River, you'll be on foot, but that rewards with its own pleasures.

This area is so beautiful that you'll feel like you're stepping into a natural paradise. Nearby is Buffalo Bay, with a scattering of small houses and a wonderful skyline. Clinging to the tip of an isthmus, there's a simple but very friendly youth hostel known as Wild Side Backpackers. It's managed by two young experts who know everything there is to know about the area and often act as impromptu guides. The hostel isn't luxurious by any means, but you'll love the atmosphere. There are endless excursions you can take, all absolutely fascinating and superbly exciting. You'll have fun shooing the Pacific gulls in the bay, and stopping for a chat with the local fishermen each morning is something of a tradition as well. You can also buy some of their wonderfully fresh fish. All while luxuriating in the sheer beauty of this enchanting spot.

Opposite: Waves break along the beach at Goukamma.
Above: The protected flora in the area is truly extraordinary. Right: Red rocks peep out of the sand.

CALA MITJIANA
MENORCA

In Menorca, the natural landscape is protected by very specific rules. There are dry stone walls and tiny lanes running down to the sea. A beach's capacity is decided by the number of spots in its car park. Not more than 50, 100, or, at most, 150 cars. It's one way of controlling the influx of visitors. At the entrances, signs light up to tell you whether you can continue on or not. This is all designed to ensure that these enchanted little corners remain just that, even at the height of the summer rush. A UNESCO Biosphere Reserve since 1993, the most secluded of the Balearic Islands has 134 miles of coastline and an elegant string of bays and rocky nooks and crannies. Cala Mitjiana is down a rather tricky dirt road about 4 miles outside Ferreries: first follow the signs for Cala Galdana and then turn left. It's an absolutely must-see for anyone vacationing on Menorca. The best time to go is in the morning when it's still deserted. Silky soft sand, a turquoise sea, and 300 feet of seashore backed by cool woodland await you. Its status as a former British dominion, and the disciplined approach of the local people themselves, means that tourism here is refreshingly sustainable. Nudism is restricted to just a few areas. Take the lane out of Mitjiana to the right and you'll quickly come upon another heavenly sight: Cala Mitjianeta, a cove beautifully sheltered from both sea and wind and thus ideal for mooring boats. If you go left, you'll find Cala Trebeluger, which isn't quite as blue but is very private. Peregrine falcons nest on the cliffs, and the caves along the shore are populated by bats and frogs. Menorca is a sporty island (cycling, trekking, golf, sailing, diving) but the horse reigns supreme—the paths that crisscross the island are wonderful for hacking, and there are races, too.

NEARBY

Son Catlar is a 15-acre Talaiot village dating back to 1400 BC. Menorca has lots of fine archaeology for visitors. Its treasures include the megalithic **Naveta des Tudons** between Ferrieres and Ciutadella: this burial place is Europe's oldest intact construction dating back to 3500 BC, with 100 human remains found there. Another visit not to miss is **Ciutadella**, a canal port lined by sandstone buildings, which bursts into life on June 23 and 24 for the feast of Saint John, when the famous "battle of the hazelnuts" takes place. *Pomada* (gin and lemonade) flows freely at this festival, too!

Above: Cala Mitjianeta, a beach just a few minutes away from Cala Mitjiana. **Right**: *The stunning Cala Mitjiana: its visitor numbers are strictly limited on a daily basis to protect it.*

The glorious Venice Lido has hosted the Venice International Film Festival for the last 70 years while its historic Hotel des Bains provided the sublime backdrop for Luchino Visconti's eerily atmospheric 1971 movie version of Thomas Mann's classic, *Death in Venice*. Who could resist the secret allure of the Promenade des Planches at Deauville, a celebrity showcase since Coco Chanel opened her first store there in 1913? Then, Utah Beach in Normandy, stage to the Allied Landing on D-Day on June 6, 1944. Each so different but powerfully unique. A once-in-a-lifetime experience. In a word: legendary.

Luca Liguori

LEGENDARY
beaches

IPANEMA
RIO DE JANEIRO

R io de Janeiro's beaches are like an extension of home for the Carioca (locals) and
tourists alike, and where the two worlds meet. The beach is marked out by numbered
lifeguard towers with fresh water showers and bars and specific areas for different
social groups. There is, for instance, a stretch of beach reserved for Gls (gays, lesbians, and
sympathizers) and one for latter-day hippies. There are also sections where Rio's well-heeled
youngsters congregate and another for sports fanatics. Women rule at Copacabana: they're
adored, flirted with, and adulated. More intellectual types prefer Ipanema as it provided the
inspiration for Vinicius de Moraes' legendary *Garota de Ipanema* (*The Girl from Ipanema*),
a tale of platonic love between a gorgeous but lonely girl and her shy admirer. Ipanema is
a trendy, chic spot, but it's also wonderfully democratic, varied, and fun. Little kiosks sell
coconut water, caipirinha, lime, sugar, Cachaça (a liquor made from fermented sugar cane),
and ice. Jogging, playing soccer, and feasting your eyes on the perfect physiques of the young
Carioca and the beautiful seas are just a few of the things to do at Ipanema. Savor the sunset
and views of the Morro Dois Irmãos (Two Brothers' Hill) from Arpoador Rock. The show
goes on nonstop, day and night. There's no closing time here. Ever. The highpoint of the
Ipanema calendar is New Year's Eve, when thousands of people dressed in white (the color of
peace) gather on the beach to leave offerings to the goddess of the sea, Iemanjá. Only when
the gifts have been borne out to sea by the currents is the goddess deemed to be satisfied and
the Carioca can look forward to a prosperous new year.

NEARBY

Legend has it that God lavished two of the seven days
he took to create the world on shaping Rio alone.
This easy-going city throbs with a permanent vacation
atmosphere despite being home to 8 million people,
with its 56 miles of white sandy beaches. Gazing down
over the city from his perch on the top of the Corcovado
and enclosing it in a divine embrace is the statue of
Cristo Redentor. The views from there are breath-taking.
On the opposite side of Guanabara Bay is the **Sugar
Loaf**. So what else do you need: a white sandy beach,
and a glass of caipirinha to relax the mind.

*Above: The Carioca work out in an open-air gym on Ipanema Beach. **Right:** Ipanema Beach and, behind
the skyscrapers, the Lagoa Rodrigo de Freitas lagoon.*

ANAKENA BEACH
RAPA NUI

Rapa Nui, better known as Easter Island, the cradle of a civilization whose origins remain a mystery, lies 2,300 miles off the northern coast of Chile, making it one of the most remote islands in the world. Rapa Nui is a tiny 100-square-mile triangle of land adrift in the Pacific Ocean inhabited by just a few thousand people. It has a subtropical climate with temperatures holding steady at around 71°F, which means you can visit all year round. However, this small corner of paradise on earth is also home to the even more heavenly Anakena Beach, which is actually inside the Rapa Nui National Park that was founded in 1935. You'll need to buy a ticket to enter the park in Orongo, a town in the south of the island. Full of caves, *ahu* (ancient ceremonial platforms), *moai* (statues), the ruins of ancient villages, and rock engravings, this is a truly stunning nature reserve. Anakena looks like a gorgeous Polynesian beach: a long strip of white sand and powdery coral lapped by a warm, crystalline sea, while the rest of Rapa Nui's coastline is all black rock.

According to local legend it was here that the first peoples landed from the Marquesas Islands. Rapa Nui (big Rapa in Polynesian) is famous for its mysterious *moai*, gigantic carved stone heads scattered across the island like a superb open-air museum. Anakena is perfect for snorkeling and sunbathing and for its sheer beauty. It is also flanked by two of the world's most important archaeological sites: Ahu Ature Huki and Nau Nau, both restored in 1954, which bear witness to Anakena's ancient origins (the settlement here was founded by the first King of Rapa Nui, Ariki Hotu Matua). Kevin Reynolds shot the film *Rapa Nui* on the beach in 1994. Rapa Nui is an eco-tourism destination and since 2008 has been a "special territory" enjoying greater independence from Chile.

NEARBY

Hanga Roa with its colorful houses and **Ahu Akivi** with its 7 *moai* gazing out over the sea both deserve a visit. The **Ahu Te Pito Kura** archaeological site and the **Rano Raraku**, where there are more than 400 *moai* from different eras, including one standing 67 feet high, are both near the beach. From this part of the island, you can also see the *motu* (little islands) of **Kao Kao, Iti,** and **Nui**, which is where the annual competition to collect the first egg of *manutara* (sooty tern) was once held. Hiking, horse trekking, diving, sport fishing, and photography safaris are available throughout the island.

*Above: The dream-like beach at Anakena is completely wild and unspoilt. **Right**: A herd of horses on Rapa Nui with the iconic Easter Island heads lined up along the cliff behind them.*

BELLES RIVES
PROVENCE

NEARBY

Old Antibes. Juan-les-Pins and Antibes are two sides of the same coin: beach on the one hand and the long history of an ancient little citadel founded by the Greeks on the other. Take a pleasant stroll along the narrow streets of old Antibes—you'll find that some are lively and busy, others silent and solitary. The **Cours Massena** market is a wonderful portrait of Provence. After that, walk up to the Grimaldi Castle, home to the **Picasso Museum**, where there are some fine works made between 1945 and 1949. Picasso spent three months here in 1946. The most emblematic of the works he produced during his time in Antibes is *La joie de vivre*, a wonderful celebration of the Mediterranean vitality of that particular period in his career.

There are few sights to compare with the beauty of the Bay of La Napoule enclosed by the Esterel hills and dotted with the Lérins Islands. It's no coincidence that Juan-les-Pins, and the villas and hotels of Cap d'Antibes, have been one of the favorite haunts of the international jet set for almost a century. In 1925 Zelda and Scott Fitzgerald set up home in the Villa Saint Louis, which a few years later became the Hotel Belles Rives. It was there that the legendary American writer began one of his most famous novels, *Tender Is the Night*, which is set in this part of the Côte d'Azur and whose characters were based directly on the wild party-goers of the day. This was the start of the *années folles* that saw the Cap reach the peak of its fame: Rudolph Valentino and Mistinguett, John Dos Passos and Vittorio Emanuele Orlando, Ernest Hemingway and La Belle Otero all flocked here as did kings, queens, and aristocrats from around the world.

Ladies discarded their dresses for the first time and slid into the water in bathing suits. This was also when the "summer season" began. Previously, the Riviera was just a place where the European aristocracy wintered. Going to the Belles Rives is like taking a trip down memory lane: the mosaics in the hall, the pale wood furniture, the Fitzgerald bar, the old elevator, the room numbers, the atmosphere in the La Passagère restaurant all remain very 1930s. The private beach as well seems like a plunge back into the past, but it's a great place for a dip in the water or to rent watersports equipment. The blue and white striped canopies, the sun umbrellas, and the comfortable sun loungers all cry out for a good book, a long chat, or something delicious to nibble on. The terrace is enchanting in the evenings with its backdrop of bougainvillea and maritime pines. Juan-les-Pins—the name is not misleading. La Pinède Gould is just behind the Hotel Belles Rives and has hosted Europe's oldest and most magical jazz festival every year since 1960.

Above: A view of the Golfe Juan from the Hotel Belles Rives. **Opposite:** *Sun loungers, beach umbrellas, and tables on the Hotel Belles Rives' sun terrace.*

FRANCE

PAMPELONNE
PROVENCE

Pampelonne is one of the most famous beaches in the world and although it actually belongs to the municipality of Ramatuelle, its name is more often associated with glitzy Saint-Tropez which is just a couple of miles away. It achieved celebrity status in the 1950s after it featured in director Roger Vadim's *And God Created Woman*. This is credited as the movie that launched Brigitte Bardot's career and was shot in 1955 amid the fishermen's cottages of Saint-Tropez, and on the then-deserted beach of Pampelonne. This was also where the legend of Club 55 was born after Vadim asked the owner of a *cabanon* on the beach to make meals for him, his wife Brigitte, and the crew during filming. As a result, this private house turned into one of the chicest clubs of the day. Celebrity couple Alain Delon and Mireille Darc lived there as well and Mick Jagger and Bianca married hippy-style on the beach in 1971. There are still free and nudist sections, but it is also home to several popular hangouts such as the Tahiti Plage, which used the bamboo sets from a 1935 film, *Aloha, Le Chant des Iles*, when it opened. Robert de Niro, Jack Nicholson, Sylvester Stallone, and George W. Bush were all also regulars at the legendary Club Voile Rouge, which happened to be Grace Kelly's favorite cocktail spot. Pampelonne still retains much of its unspoilt natural beauty. Its lovely dunes provide a gentle habitat for many rare plants, such as nettle-leafed figwort, forget-me-nots, and woundwort. However, you'll see these more easily off-season when this enchanting beach is as lonely as it was before it was "discovered," with solitary herds of sheep wandering its shores.

NEARBY

Take the time to explore the fortified village of **Ramatuelle**. It's a charming labyrinth of alleyways, arches, steps, and lovely ochre houses with flower-filled balconies. The old **Saracen Port** is intact while the Romanesque **Church of Notre-Dame** still has its lovely 17th-century portal and Baroque altar pieces. Don't miss the local Provencale market on Thursday and Sunday in the **Place de l'Ormeau**. One of the legends of French cinema, Gérard Philippe, is also buried in the village cemetery. In July and August, there are classical, light, and jazz music festivals in Ramatuelle as well.

Above: Pampelonne Beach is near Ramatuelle and still retains all the charm and understated sophistication of the Côte d'Azur itself. Right: The beguiling port of Saint-Tropez shot by Gianni Berengo Gardin.

PROMENADE DES PLANCHES
NORMANDY

The history of the beach at Deauville, a gorgeous little seaside town in the heart of Normandy, is linked with a host of famous names. It is snobbish, intellectual, and the perfect place for people who love being by the sea out of season. In the past, Deauville has attracted the likes of Coco Chanel (she opened her first boutique here in 1913). Scott Fitzgerald, Ian Fleming, and Josephine Baker, as well as numerous aristocrats and members of the Parisian beau monde. This is, after all, the legendary capital of the Normandy Riviera. In the days of Louis Philippe, the nearby fishing village of Trouville became France's chicest coastal resort, but Deauville owes its fame to Napoleon III's half-brother, the Duke of Morny. In 1858, he decided to create a "kingdom of elegance" out of nothing on the other side of the river Touques, which acted as a de facto border with Trouville. The duke's ambition was to replace the huge expanse of sand and marshy waters with a sophisticated miniature Paris that would be considered nothing less than the 21st arrondissement (quarter). Located just a couple of hours from the French capital, Deauville quickly became a marvel in its own right, burgeoning with luxury fin de siècle villas (don't miss the Villa Strassburger), its long sandy beach, and the Promenade des Planches, edged with the famous *planches* (wooden boardwalk). Another feature that makes Deauville's beach unique these days, however, is that you can horse trek right along the shore.

Naturally enough, we shouldn't forget that the town also hosts the American Film Festival each year in September. Deauville owes part of its charm to its unusual beach huts painted with the names of Hollywood stars. High-profile movies have also been shot here including *Coco Avant Chanel* (*Coco Before Chanel*) and *A Man and a Woman*, starring Jean-Louis Trintignant and Anouk Aimée (winner of the Palm d'Or at Cannes in 1966 as well as 2 Oscars). Director Claude Lelouch recently returned there after 45 years to make *Ces amours-là*, an homage to Deauville and its long beach.

NEARBY

Marcel Proust, Alexander Dumas, and Marguerite Duras all vacationed at **Trouville**, and always spent time at the Hotel des Roches Noires. However, only distant echoes of those glory days remain today. But in nearby **Cabourg**, room number 414 in the Grand Hotel, once occupied by Marcel Proust, has survived. **Honfleur** (7 miles away) has nice narrow streets, old houses, and a port immortalized by the Impressionists. Another artists' favorite is **Etretat**, 37 miles away, whose white cliffs Monet painted—a spectacular spot to watch the sun go down over the Atlantic. There are also plenty of picturesque chateaus including **Auge** and **Normandy Barrière**.

*Above: The beautiful Promenade des Planches beach. **Opposite:** The lovely wooden boardwalk that runs along the promenade at Deauville beach.*

UTAH BEACH
NORMANDY

Utah Beach is the most famous of the 5 Normandy beaches on which the Allies landed under the command of General Eisenhower on D-Day, June 6, 1944. Around 20,000 men, 1,700 vehicles, and 1,700 tons of munitions came ashore that day as the tide literally turned against the Nazis. Utah Beach runs along the Cotentin peninsula in the municipality of Sainte-Marie-du-Mont and Saint-Martin-de-Varreville. It has been celebrated in dozens of war films, including Steven Spielberg's *Saving Private Ryan*. This is a place alive with memories and it's also home to a museum commemorating the historic landings. Blending nicely into the surrounding landscape, the Musée du Debarquement (Landings Museum) was built in 1961 around an old bunker and has been given huge windows that flood it with natural light. This is a highly symbolic place, and the Normandy landings have been recreated here in absolutely meticulous detail using a scale model. There are also hundreds of film clips, memorabilia, and documents from the time as well as photographs, slides, and an exceptional film library. The little country roads all around Utah Beach are lined with banks thick with roots, bushes, and trees. It's easy to imagine how exhausted the soldiers must have been as they trudged along with large packs on their backs, often engaging in hand-to-hand combat. Then you see the dunes and the legendary beach itself where the soldiers dodged enemy fire as they struggled to get out of the water. Walking there now you'll hear the sound of the sea, but you only have to close your eyes to imagine the noise and confusion of that terrible yet historic day. Before you leave the area, don't forget stop at Café Roosevelt: the walls are covered with the signatures of veterans who come here with their children and grandchildren.

NEARBY

Sainte Mère Elise is a village filled with reminders of the liberation of France. Its little square is famous because it was here where the parachute regiments landed—a scene depicted in the film *The Longest Day*. Then there is **Colleville**, with its hundreds of white crosses and Stars of David. At **Omaha Beach**, also known as Bloody Omaha, you'll see the dunes where the Germans slaughtered Allied troops. **Bayeux** is a gorgeous town in Calvados with the lovely museum housing the **Tapisserie de la Reine Mathilde**, a 220-foot-long tapestry depicting the exploits of William the Conqueror in his conquest of England.

Above: The long expanse of sand at Utah Beach is perfect for horse racing. Right: There are many gull colonies all along the fascinating and seemingly endless Utah Beach.

MARINA BEACH
TAMIL NADU

NEARBY

The **Kamarajar Salai**, a major artery that runs parallel to Marina Beach, is lined with old colonial buildings from the days of the British Raj, resplendent in the morning light. The most notable of these are the **University of Madras**, **Chepauk Palace,** and **Vivekananda House**, the latter hosting art exhibitions and other shows dedicated to the life and times of the eponymous Hindu monk. There's also a hugely popular aquarium nearby that's home to a stunning array of tropical sea and fresh water fish. Last but not least, the **lighthouse** at the very southern tip of the beach is worth a visit—climb it and you'll have the multicolored city of Chennai unfold at your feet.

They say that Marina Beach is a legendary place but then so is India itself. Maybe it's something to do with its long, history of art, culture, and tradition, maybe it's the spirituality that pervades every aspect of everyday life, or maybe it's the fact that it has been reborn from the tsunami that devastated it in 2004.

Joie de vivre reigns supreme in this wonderful part of the world, a place where the perfume of sandalwood and jasmine hangs in the air, blending with spices. A place where dawn and dusk ignite the endless expanse of golden sand against the tempestuous waters of the bay while brilliant saris turn women into sensuous goddesses as they saunter along its length. Located near the city of Chennai on the east coast of the state of Tamil Nadu, Marina Beach earned its legendary status because of its size—it stretches an amazing 7.5 miles. There's room here for everything and everyone: for the fishing communities that live on either end, for the people that jog or horse-ride along it, for the children playing cricket, and even for the kites that whirl in a colorful haze above it. Swimming isn't advisable at Marina Beach because the waves are very powerful and there are strong undertows as well, but great hang gliding and windsurfing do attract scores of adventure-lovers. As evening approaches the beach and boardwalk gradually take on a wonderfully exotic and old-fashioned festival atmosphere as vendors selling fruit juice, shells, glass balls, kites, and the spicy local foods dot the crowds. Farther inland, between the palms and horsetail trees, you can see imposing stone statues of famous figures, from Mahatma Gandhi to Thiruvalluvar, Sir Thomas Munro, Kamarajar, and Periyar. There's also Anna Square, the mausoleum of Minister Annadurai, and the splendid park named in honor of the politician and actor M. G. Ramachandran, all people who are dear to the hearts of ordinary Indians and make up a part of the legend of this exotic country.

Above: A woman selling local snacks and produce at Marina Beach. **Opposite:** *The colors of Marina Beach, which is thronged, night and day, by fishermen.*

OM BEACH
KARNATAKA

At sunset when the sky and sea touch along the horizon, the beach at Gokarna is a genuinely magical place. The warm light lends the sand and rocks a pinkish hue, caressing the blue outline of the fishing boats. On Om Beach—named after the om symbol made by its slivers of sand—the last hippies to flee thronged Goa. Here, they meditate cross-legged, their eyes half-closed, their faces turned to the Arabian Sea. Nearby, groups of girls practice yoga, their limbs gently gliding through the air. A few black cows casually wander along the beach unheeded. A bar with a straw roof offers beer and hammocks. The scene is set to retrieve that lost sense of harmony and balance that Westerners seek in the East. Gokarna, "the cow's ear" in the local language, is located in southwest India and is one of the most sacred Hindu sites on the entire subcontinent. Cows symbolize *dharma*, or cosmic order, and so just coming here is considered propitious. There's also Swaswara, a chic wellness resort overlooking the beach where guests practice yoga and receive ayurveda, the science of long life. Plenty of boats are available to take you from Om Beach to little sandy coves nearby and to the port into which fishing trawlers chug each day with their catch. A lively, colorful spectacle. Gokarna is also a place of pilgrimage, particularly in February and March for the Feast of Shivaratri, which celebrates the night that Shiva performed her cosmic dance. The red dirt main street is where it all happens, and it is lined with shops selling bracelets and necklaces. In fact, the road ends on Gokarna beach. All along the shore you'll see women busy washing their flame-colored saris and shaven-headed pilgrims taking their ritual dip in the sea.

NEARBY

Apart from its beaches, Gokarna also has many ancient temples along its main roads and in the surrounding hills. The **Temples of Mahabaleshwar,** with its sacred lingam, **Ganati** dedicated to Ganesh, **Venkataraman** with its large ablutions pool, and **Rama** overlooking the beach are worth a visit. All reveal an extremely spiritual India, very far removed from the tourist frenzy of Goa and the high-tech buzz of Bangalore, the region's capital. Go farther south and you'll find magnificent beaches and fishing villages. If you press on all the way to **Karkal** and **Mudabidri,** you'll find fine temples as well.

*Above: It's not unusual to see groups of people practicing yoga or meditating on Om Beach. **Right:** Indian women busy washing their saris on the shore at Om Beach.*

PURI

ORISSA

A sacred city for Indian Hindus and a place of pilgrimage for centuries, Puri hosts grandiose festivals and has a fantastic beach. Right in the very center of town is the Jagannath Temple, which non-Hindus cannot enter. Here begins the Rath Yatra Festival, during which the faithful drag 45-foot-high sculptures of Jagannath, "Lord of the Universe," along on chariots (*rath*). Even the British colonialists were so impressed with the sight of the festival that they coined the term "juggernaut" to indicate anything colossal or unstoppable. The city of Puri has a population of 160,000 and is the capital of the eponymous district in the state of Orissa, which hugs the Bay of Bengal and extends over 300 miles along the east coast. Around 5 million people live in Orissa and are divided into no less than 62 ethnic and religious groups, each one with its own ancient customs and rituals.

The majestic 12th-century Jagannath Temple is surrounded by a very high wall that provides protection for other smaller temples. Legend has it that anyone who prays here for 3 days and 3 nights will be freed from the cycle of reincarnation. During the joyous, exhausting Rath Yatra, the huge wooden statues are dragged through the streets on chariots by literally thousands of Hindu devotees in honor of the voyage made by Jagannath, to the temple of Gundicha, aunt of Krishna, where he remains for a week before returning to his own temple. While the Temple of Jagannath is reserved strictly for Hindus, the festivals and the beaches are open to everyone, including the Puri Beach Festival, which is celebrated in early November each year. The fine white sandy shore at Puri isn't one of those beaches you stretch out on with your sun umbrella and a cocktail, however. It is frequented mostly by Indians. This is a beach that's all about long strolls and plenty of stop-offs for refreshments at the tea and coconut stalls en route. You'll enjoy meeting the local fishermen, who are happy to ferry tourists about at sea. There are also plenty of superb masseurs. Both dawn

NEARBY

Nature-lovers will adore the area around Puri. We recommend you start with **Chilika**, a huge lake dotted with tiny islands and home to a wide variety of aquatic species. In winter, in fact, birds migrate here from as far as Siberia. There are also lots of national parks, including **Similipal,** which is home to the Barehipani Waterfalls, and **Balighai**, a center for sea turtle research. **Ananda Bazar** is an enormous produce market, and **Balighai Beach**, at the mouth of the river Nuanai, is a great place for picnics. For crafts, visit the famous villages of **Pipli** and **Raghurajpur**, where you'll find sophisticated handicrafts from the Orissa region on display and for sale.

Opposite: A mystical atmosphere imbues the beach at Puri in the soft evening light. **Left:** *Fishermen taking in their nets on the sandy shore.*

and dusk here call for religious venerations. As the sun sinks below the horizon, the beach comes alive with fishermen dragging
in their boats, nets, lines, and boxes. As the pinkish-purple light of
dawn breaks, the faithful dip themselves into the purifying waters
at Swargdwar Beach as the waves glitter and ripple around them.
This is an *ashram* overlooking the ocean, a place of meditation, a
time of transmission of divine grace for anyone moved by the sense
of sacredness of this centuries-old sun worship.

The best time of year to visit Puri is between October and
March when temperatures range between 59 and a balmy 77°F. If
you go in June or July for the Rath Yatra, you'll have a bit of a battle
with the humidity and temperatures that exceed 95°F.

Above: *Boats hauled up ashore on Puri beach make a colorful sight.*
Right: *Diligent regulars on the beach at Puri.*

DAYANG BUNTING

LANGKAWI

A long sliver of white sand curling along the emerald waters of the Andaman Sea, just north of Malaysia, Palau Dayang Bunting is one of only 4 inhabited islands in the Langkawi Archipelago, which numbers 99 in all (104 at low tide). It's a place that has captivated visitors at first sight. Nature reigns supreme here, with mangrove swamps and steep rocky basalt cliffs covered with lush jungle vegetation. This is an incredibly sensual, lively part of the world. The surrounding seas have spawned a host of legends and myths. Dayang Bunting was reputedly one of the resting places of Garuda, the eagle of Lord Vishnu. Even today, magnificent sea eagles whirl in the sky as they search out their next prey from the 53 species of fish that populate the local sea and rivers. The shallow waters just along Dayang Bunting's shoreline also teem with brilliantly colored fish. If you leave the beach for a while and make your way inland, you'll be immersed in a truly magical atmosphere full of carnivorous plants. Palau Dayang Bunting has so much going for it: you can chill out on the white sandy beach, swim in the warm, clear sea, snorkel along the seafloor, and take a delicious dip in the famous fresh water Lake of the Pregnant Maiden farther inland. There is a platform with a ladder to allow visitors to dive in the green depths of this propitious lake. It is a favorite place to swim for couples hoping to start a family, since according to an ancient local legend the princess and nymph Mambang Sari and her husband Mat Teja, pretender to the kingdom of Langkawi, conceived an heir after drinking its waters. Unfortunately, the child didn't survive for long and its heartbroken parents threw its body into the lake. Since then the local people have believed that the lake waters are a source of fertility and also that only the pure of heart can see the baby's reflection in its gleaming waters. The lake itself has many little inlets and is located in the heart of a nature reserve.

NEARBY

The **Gua Langsir** or Cave of the Banshee, which is home to thousands of bats, is a good trek from the lake. In Langkawi (18 miles south), you can snorkel in the **Palau Payar Marine Reserve**. The main island also has a marine observation chamber 1 mile offshore. Don't miss the fantastic eagle feeding tour (by boat). There is also a very interesting 39-foot-high stone eagle on the Langkawi shoreline. Go to **Pantal Cenang** for the wonderfully white beaches and **Makam Mahsuri**, a marble mausoleum erected in memory of the wife of the son of the King of Langkawi, who was executed for adultery and from whose wounds white blood flowed.

Opposite: Dayang Bunting beach and the Langkawi Archipelago. **Left**: Fishing is very much part of the culture in Malaysia. The locals often stick to traditional methods as the seas are so rich in fish.

CALA D'ARENA
SARDINIA

Until a few years ago, only the few residents of Asinara had the privilege of admiring Cala d'Arena. Sadly, most of those were either inmates or guards at the island's legendary maximum security prison. This was nothing less than Italy's very own Alcatraz and home to the infamous likes of mafia bosses Totò Riina and Raffaele Cutolo. Further back in history, sailors suffering from serious contagious disease were quarantined in the island's Lazzaretto, founded in 1885. Also built at the time was the famous penal colony, which doubled as a prisoner of war camp during both world wars. Neither prisoners nor patients would have been in the mood to appreciate the allure of Asinara and Cala d'Arena. But no one else was allowed on the island as it was completely off-limits to the public. It was only in 1997, when it was made a national park, that people were allowed access. They traveled over by motorboat out of Stintino or Porto Torres or in their own private craft, having gained special permission from the Parks Board.

Cala d'Arena is actually a paradise within a paradise. In winter, it is split in two by a rainwater stream, which makes it particularly fascinating. Its incredibly white sand and clear waters have earned it the name of "Maldives of the Mediterranean." It has magnificent rocky areas but is ringed by lush Mediterranean brush out of which you might see the occasional albino donkey, and is crowned by a 17th-century Aragonese watchtower. The breathtakingly gorgeous Cala d'Arena is completely protected by law: while you are free to look, you should leave no trace when you visit. This is an incomparably perfect beach. Even Italian judges Giovanni Falcone and Paolo Borsellino spent time here preparing their huge and legendary case against the Sicilian mafia, which would unfortunately cost both of them their lives in 1992.

NEARBY

The northern area of Asinara, which is home to Cala d'Arena, is the most glorious part of the island. If you hike, you'll see breathtaking vistas open up before you. Alternatively, you can rent a bike on the dockside and visit the **Elighe Mannu Botanical Observatory** or **Punta Scomunica** which, at 1,300 ft., really does afford unparalleled views. You could also bike to **La Reale**, former location of the Lazzaretto and the Savoy Royal Family palace. **Cala d'Oliva** is close by: it once was home to a prison village with offices, church, school, workshop, carpentry shop, and cheese-making dairy. And don't miss the **Punta Scorno** lighthouse.

*Above: The prison on Asinara closed in 1997 when the island was declared a national park. **Opposite:** The lovely rounded shape of Cala d'Arena.*

CASTELFUSANO

LAZIO

There's a stretch of sea just a stone's throw from Rome that has become part of the collective imagination of movie lovers because its dunes appeared in numerous Italian movies made in the 1960s and 1970s. This 3-mile stretch of coast extends from Ostia to Anzio and is known as Castelfusano beach. Hugged by the Via Litoranea (Coast Road), it has provided the backdrop to great Italian actors like Vittorio Gassman, Alberto Sordi, Marcello Mastroianni, Gigi Proietti, and Ugo Tognazzi. One movie in particular—Sergio Citti's *Casotto* (1977)—was set in and around the beach huts that line the Roman waterfronts. Dipping in the waters of Castelfusano in that movie were not only Proietti and Tognazzi, but Catherine Deneuve, Mariangela Melato, Paolo Stoppa, and Michele Placido. There was even a cameo from a very fresh-faced Jodie Foster, whose lines were dubbed into the gutsy local dialect for the occasion. Castelfusano is just 16 miles from Rome by road. Then you take Via Cristoforo Colombo and once you've gone through the pine wood, turn left and you'll reach the dunes and Mediterranean brush. The first stretch of beach you meet is Castelporziano, and is strictly off-limits to bathers because it's part of the president of Italy's private residence. It is followed by 8 "gates" leading onto the beach itself. The very tip of Castelporziano beach is known as Capocotta and is a naturist area. Here, in 1953, the body of a woman named Wilma Montesi was discovered, causing a huge sensation in the press and driving the paparazzi into a frenzy. The whole sordid episode provided the inspiration for Federico Fellini's *La Dolce Vita*.

NEARBY

Diving and snorkeling fans will absolutely adore Castelfusano because of the nearby **Secche di Tor Paterno** marine reserve, a submerged island lying 80 feet below. This is a wonderful place to see coral and the local posidonia seaweed. Don't miss the archaeological excavations at **Ostia Antica**, just a few miles from the beach. They've revealed a lost city dating back to the 4th century BC whose foundations are still perfectly preserved to this day. The site corresponds to the location of the old port of Rome where the Tiber flowed into the Tyrrhenian Sea.

*Above: Powdery white sandy beach stretches as far as the eye can see at Castelfusano. **Right:** The lush colors of the Mediterranean scrub hugs the coast at Castelfusano beach.*

VENICE LIDO
VENETO

With its links to the jet set, literature, and film, the elegant Lido is every bit as legendary as the city of Venice itself. The Lido Island is now synonymous with the annual Venice Film Festival, but the real appeal of this strip of land nestled between the lagoon and the Adriatic is its long sandy beach and the elegant bathing complexes that line it. The first of these was built on Santa Elisabetta beach in 1857, marking the start of a period of rapid development for the Lido. Northern European–style *capanne* or beach huts were introduced in 1895—they're perfect places to have lunch, take shelter from the sun, and play cards. Each private bathing complex is painted a different color, and the charming little wooden huts also have canopies and verandas, so that guests can feel entirely at home and at ease. One of the Lido's most famous guests was Lord Byron, who adored swimming out to the island where he kept his horses. The philosopher Arthur Schopenhauer actually wrote that he saw the English poet riding along the beach one day in 1819. The Lido's rich international clientele also came for the luxury hotels. The Art Nouveau Hotel des Bains, which opened its doors in 1900, became a favorite with international aristocracy like choreographer Sergej Djagilev, while the Moorish-inspired Excelsior Palace (1908) was popular with millionaires and adventurers. Thomas Mann's masterpiece *Death in Venice* immortalized the Hotel des Bains and the beach in front of it. Years later the German writer noted: "There is no better sea to bathe in and the nearness of a city like Venice makes the whole place unique." The decadent beauty of the Lido's locations and characters from Mann's novella were made into a movie by Luchino Visconti in 1971 with Gustav Mahler's Third and Fourth Symphonies as a soundtrack. The Lido's legend lives on now with the Venice International Film Festival, which attracts the crème de la crème of the film world to Italy's most evocative city each year. The gala dinner that opens the event is also held here, and the beach has provided the backdrop for endless photo shoots.

NEARBY

There is more to Lido Island than just the area around the Church of Santa Maria Elisabetta, the eponymous boulevard, and luxury Art Nouveau hotels and villas. There are some very intimate corners such as **Malamocco**, in the southern part of the island, the location of one of the first settlements in Venice's lagoon. It still has a majestic fort, the Podestà's Palace and the Church of Santa Maria Assunta. **Pellestrina** island is a 7-mile stretch of land between sea and lagoon with colorful houses and beautiful natural sites. The nearby **Ca' Roman** Lido offers 100 acres of beach, dunes, and Mediterranean brush too. Don't miss **San Pietro in Volta** and its beautifully frescoed church.

Opposite: The Venice Lido in front of the former Excelsior Palace, now the Grand Hotel Excelsior. **Left**: The Lido's beach and its famous wooden huts.

NEARBY

Just outside the village of Xaghra at the back of Ramla Bay lies the **Temples of Ggantija**, spectacular megalithic monuments which, according to legend, were built by a giantess. You'll also come across three incredible sights of nature at **Dwejra** on the island's west coast: **il-Qawra**, the Inland Sea, which runs into the open sea through a fissure in the rock; **Fungus Rock** (il-Gebla tal-General); and **Tieqa Zerqa**, an enormous arch of stone known as the blue window. Nature reigns supreme on Gozo: the aim is to turn the whole island into a model of sustainability and environmental protection by 2015. Ramla Bay is also the focus of a protection program managed by the Maltese Gaia foundation.

Ramla il-Hamra: the "beach of the red sand"—there's a heroic ring to that name. And well there might be. Ramla Bay is Gozo's largest and most beautiful beach as well as being one of the most stunning anywhere in the Mediterranean. Lapped by a turquoise sea, its expanse of coral-red sand nestles between two rocky yet green promontories and backs onto dunes topped by tamarisk and bamboo. In summer it's a prime location for swimmers, sunbathers, and surfers. There are no tourist facilities here. It's very, very unspoilt with just a few little stalls selling ice cream or *gozitan ftira*, the Maltese version of pizza. Out of season, it's easy to imagine the storms unleashed by Zeus driving Ulysses' ship as far as the coast of Gozo, which is referred to as the island of Ogygia in the *Odyssey*. The Greek hero is said to have spent 7 years on the island as a "prisoner of love" of the sea nymph Calypso until his yearning to return to Ithaca grew stronger even than the lure of her promise gift of immortality she'd promised. The Cave of Calypso can be found on the western promontory of Xaghra, which dominates Ramla Bay. A series of stone steps leads down into the cave itself, which is considerably less romantic than Homer's description.

However, the mere idea of actually being at the heart of the legend is quite moving and the darkness (bring a torch!) does add a touch of mystery. The view from the promontory is also exactly the same one Ulysses himself would have gazed upon as he dreamed of his far-off isle. The ruins of a Roman villa from the Imperial era have also been discovered on the beach as have fortifications built by the legendary Knights of Malta. Right in the middle of the beach there is also a statue of the Virgin Mary. Gleaming pristine white on its pedestal in the reddish sand, it commemorates one of the many shipwrecks to have occurred in these parts and is dated 1881. Ramla Bay is a magical place and was used as the backdrop to a BBC production starring Jonny Lee Miller and Vanessa Redgrave about the life of Lord Byron, who had a great love of Maltese Islands.

*Above: The megalithic temple of Ta'Hagrat, which was made a UNESCO World Heritage Site in 1992. **Opposite:** The coral-colored sand of Ramla Bay.*

THE BEACH
KOH PHI PHI LEH

"There has to be a place, an experience, an encounter in some place in the world capable of changing what everything means," declared Leonardo di Caprio at the premier of the movie *The Beach,* based on the eponymous novel by Alex Garland and directed by Danny Boyle in 2000. Such a place—where every thought and passion is swept away by the majesty of the nature around you—really does exist in the form of Ao Maya, which was chosen as the backdrop for the most stunning scenes from the movie. As a result, it's now known simply as The Beach. A crescent of white sand tucked away on the Andaman Coast in South-East Thailand, it nestles amid the jagged western cliffs of Koh Phi Phi Leh, the smaller of the two Phi Phi Islands. After its glittering debut on the big screen, the little bay is, of course, no longer the mysterious paradise it once was. That said, however, it has lost none of its legendary beauty. It's best to arrive by sea, as it appears out of nowhere enclosed by high rocky limestone walls dripping with lush vegetation that's reflected in a turquoise lagoon. Take a dive out of the boat into the warm, velvety embrace of the shallow, crystal

NEARBY

Koh Phi Phi Leh has some surprisingly little inlets that were once used as hiding places by pirates. Two must-sees are the **Pilah Lagoon,** on the east of the island, and farther north the **Viking Cave,** which is set into the cliff wall at sea level. This is where the local nomadic sea gypsies that live on the cliffs collect sea swallow nests (which they then sell illegally to Japan for bird's nest soup) using bamboo platforms. The island's coral depths teem with an incredible variety of fish which you can see even a few yards from the shore. These include barracuda and shy leopard shark. No trip to Koh Phi Phi Leh would be complete without at least several snorkeling sessions.

Above: A Koh Phi Phi Leh resort blends in very discreetly with the surrounding landscape. *Left*: A longtail boat tied up at the shore on The Beach. *Opposite*: The rocky cliffs of Koh Phi Phi Leh plunge into the water.

clear water and you'll realize just how heavenly this place is. A few yards from the shore, you'll see nothing but the sky reflected in the sea and a few of the sea cucumbers that the locals use as the main ingredient to make a famous soup that's alleged to have aphrodisiac qualities.

Swim a little farther out and you'll see triggerfish nibbling at the coral in the wonderful, colorful world of the reef. Back ashore, the soft coral sand looks incredibly inviting—just the spot for a snooze or some sunbathing. All your troubles will melt away as The Beach works its unhurried magic. As the day wears on, you'll feel the need for a little shade. Have no fear in that regard, either. A stone's throw away, the lush tropical vegetation is tangled with white starry jasmine flowers that imbue the air with their wonderfully sweet scent. The gigantic bulbs they grow out of dot the sand. Farther on there is a gorgeous little primordial forest whose edges blur with sculptural, sharp-leafed screw-pines that feels like something straight out of *Jurassic Park*.

You might bump into a street vendor selling drinks or colorful sarongs as you wander but you won't find any permanent kiosks or stalls around here. Since it is part of the Koh Phi Phi National Park, the island isn't inhabited and is completely wild. Day trips only are permitted. You'll have to get here by longtail boat, which you can catch on Long Beach at Phi Phi Don. Small groups of a dozen or so people at a time are taken out by these lovely, slow-going colorful craft to enjoy the sights of the coast and maybe exchange a few words with the local boatmen who are very proud of their part

in protecting the park and its unspoilt nature. Half-day excursions of this kind vary in price from 400 to 650 bath and normally include rental of snorkel masks, a waterproof ocean bag for your camera, and refreshments (usually just water and fruit).

The much cheaper but also distinctly less green option is to go by motorboat. These take around 100 people at a time and the trip won't be half as enjoyable. The best alternative really is to negotiate a private trip in a longtail boat and agree with the owner to allow you to stop at The Beach a little after sunset (around 5 in the evening), when the motorboats are heading back home and the beach itself returns to its wonderful, true self.

*Opposite: A jetty for the traditional local longtail boats. Above: Inland on the Phi Phi Islands. **Right**: The Beach, truly a little piece of paradise on earth.*

BURTON BRADSTOCK
ENGLAND

On the nights with a full moon, Charlotte and her father, who live in a cottage in Bridport, search for certain species of dinosaurs by the light of their torches on the rocks and sand of the beach at Burton Bradstock. This leg of the southwest coast of England lies in Dorset, and is a place of enormous charm and natural beauty. Charlotte, who is 10, is always devastated if she has to come home without a fossil from the Jurassic. This is, after all, the Jurassic Coast, an attraction for fossil hunters since the early 19th century. It was here that the scrupulous collector Mary Anning found the first fossilized ichthyosaurus, the first plesiosaurus in 1821, and the first pterodactyl in 1828. In the summer, there's a stretch of sea here that's as beautiful as any to bathe in, but Charlotte, who wants to be a researcher when she grows up, doesn't like swimming as much as her pals. She prefers walking along the wind- and sea-hewn rocks. Near Lyme Regis, another fairy-tale little seaside town, there is a series of cliffs that are difficult to climb because there are frequent rock falls in the area. However, the detail of the rock formations that make them up is quite visible: along

NEARBY

Check out **The Hive Beach Café** in Burton Bradstock: it serves great seafood, crab, oysters, and shellfish. Moving inland, you'll come to **Evershot**, home to Summer Lodge, a tiny hotel whose wine cellar is considered one of the world's finest by *Wine Spectator* magazine. A visit to **Abbotsbury** and its Benedictine monastery dating from 1040, is a must. It also has a Swannery where 1,000 mute swans live and Subtropical Gardens and a Children's Farm. No visit to Lyme Regis would be complete without fish and chips on **the Cobb**. Visit the **Church of Saint Nicholas** and its marvelous Lawrence Whistler windows in Moreton. Clouds Hill, Lawrence of Arabia's home, is also here and he is buried in a tiny cemetery nearby.

Above: The soft, sandy beach at Burton Bradstock. **Left:** *The little port at Lyme Regis at low tide.* **Opposite:** *The promenade and charming colored houses at Lyme Regis and the Cobb.*

this stretch of coast, you can see the passage of time, from the Triassic to the Jurassic to the Cretacean.

The view from the beach is absolutely unique: around 185 million years of Earth's history is laid out in the layers of these steep rock formations. There are just 890 such historically valuable sites scattered across the globe: 689 cultural, 25 mixed, and 176 natural. Burton Bradstock and Lyme Regis belong to the last category and have been declared part of the UNESCO Jurassic Coast World Heritage Site, which gives them special protected status. The University of Southampton monitors the various stretches of coastline and publishes essential geo-guides to them.

A few short miles from this beach, tucked away amid the Dorset hills, is the birthplace of Thomas Hardy, one of the great writers on the relationship between man and nature. Hardy knew the local people very well, as he spent hours and hours walking here each day. *Jude the Obscure* and *Tess of the d'Urbervilles* are just two of his most famous novels in which Victorian convention is put to the test.

The area has been home to many legendary names. Near Dorchester, there is a little village called Moreton, home to the beguiling Church of Saint Nicholas, famous for its amazing glass windows, magnificently engraved by Lawrence Whistler. Clouds Hill, the home of Lawrence of Arabia, is also in Moreton, and the great man is buried nearby in a tiny wooden and stone cemetery. Secret agent, soldier, archaeologist, and writer, Lieutenant Colonel Thomas Edward Lawrence is renowned for his role in

the Great Arab Revolt in 1916. Such stories also have a touch of the coastal wind about them, its wild unspoilt nature, and the isolation of the people hereabouts.

The film *The French Lieutenant's Woman*, starring Meryl Streep, was also shot at Lyme Regis and was based the novel of the same name by John Fowles, another illustrious resident of the area. The long sea wall of the Cobb was where the character played by Streep used to have her romantic liaisons with the French Lieutenant amid the sea spray.

Like Hardy, Fowles spent his life here. And now Charlotte is living here, too. In the evenings, if she's been lucky that day, she'll bring home an ammonite—something to dream about as she drifts off to sleep.

*Opposite: The effects of the low tide at Lyme Regis. **Above:** The seafront at Lyme Regis. **Right:** The magnificent rock formations on the beach at Burton Bradstock.*

Elie beach is like something out of a novel by Daniel Defoe, Robert Stevenson, or a poem by Robert Burns. It was in this part of the world that Macduff hid when fleeing from Macbeth. The colors of the landscape are soft and a little austere, but there is a very direct and fascinating relationship with the sea in these parts. The tide reigns supreme and beats out the rhythm of time as it glides in and out. The retreating waters leave Elie beach dotted with shells, prawns, crabs, and little sand fish. It's north of Edinburgh in an area of Scotland known as the Kingdom of Fife, in memory of its proud past. For a thousand years, Elie was just a small cluster of houses huddled to the northwest of the ochre beach, a tiny fishing village that gradually transformed into one of Scotland's chicest locations. The homes here span the spectrum from simple traditional fishermen's cottages to opulent late 19th-century villas. Elie is a favorite vacation spot of former British Prime Minister Gordon Brown and many other politicians with young families as well as businessmen and intellectuals.

Plenty of wind and fun is guaranteed at the hands of the instructors in the village Watersports Center, which belongs to the Royal Yachting Association (RYA) and is certified by the British Adventure Activities Licensing Authority (AALA). One of Scotland's oldest pubs, the Ship Inn, built in 1582 just in front of the castle in the port, is a favorite hangout for the younger generation. Don't miss the hike up to Lady's Tower for some seal-watching. Elie recently created its own golf club, and horse riding is also available. The Kilconquhar Castle Equestrian is particularly recommended for all levels of riders.

NEARBY

Visit the little ports of **Pittenweem** and **Anstruther**, from where you can take a boat to unspoilt **May Island** with its wonderful colonies of seals and sea puffins. Anstruther is reported to have the best fish and chips in all of Great Britain. **St. Monans** church is a spectacular sight teetering high above the sea on a rocky spur. You most certainly can't leave without a visit to **St. Andrews**, home to one of Europe's oldest universities (1413). **Kellie Castle** and the **Bunker**, where Britain's Cabinet would have taken refuge in the event of a nuclear attack during the Cold War, are on the road between Elie and St. Andrews.

*Above: The craggy ruins of St. Andrews Castle dominate this stretch of the Kingdom of Fife coast. **Right**: Elie's magnificent beach in the rosy glow of sunset.*

WAIKIKI
HAWAII

S ky and sea blend together behind the "Sunset on the Beach" movie screen. Movies are shown down on Waikiki beach every month—it's quite a retro thing and open to both locals and visitors alike. As the images flow by on the screen, you'll probably find yourself wondering how many movies have been shot in this part of the globe. Waikiki Beach is one of the world's most famous beaches and an elegant suburb of Honolulu. It's the very heart of Hawaii and very much more than just a beach. It's a huge open-air natural movie set, an almost 2-mile long stage on which people of all ages and ethnic groups act out various scenes from everyday life. You'll see muscle-bound men straight out of *Big Wednesday* (which was actually shot in California), gorgeous girls, young amber-skinned Polynesians, and surfing, surfing, surfing. Mixed in with them are older folk playing chess and couples on romantic vacations. There are always hordes of Japanese in the designer boutiques and stores. But the endless array of things to do and buy just off this golden beach shouldn't make you forget that the "gushing fountain" (a literal translation of the Hawaiian word referring to the springs and streams that separated the beach from the inland areas) affords views that are both dream-like and legendary. Diamond Head, for instance, instantly brings to mind Elvis Presley and *Blue Hawaii*. A police officer reminds you of Tom Selleck in *Magnum P.I.* Even the lifeguards seem to have walked straight off the set of *Baywatch* (many of the episodes were shot in the islands, in fact). And then there's the history enclosed in the walls of hotels like the Moana Surfrider and the Royal Hawaiian. The latter, with its huge ornate pink facade, is where the United States Pacific Command was stationed during World War II.

NEARBY

Just a few minutes outside Waikiki is **Hanauma Bay**, which provided the backdrop to the songs and cinematic loves of Elvis Presley. On the opposite coast, at Honolulu, there's the lush green **Kualoa Ranch,** where the likes of *Lost* and *Jurassic Park* were shot. Farther to the north you'll come across the **Polynesian Cultural Center**, while North Shore and Haleiwa really are ruled by surfing and surfers. Nearer to Honolulu, you'll find the **World War II monument** to those who lost their lives in the attack on Pearl Harbor and the visitor center at the Dole Plantation, for the "pineapple experience."

*Above: An iconic view of the legendary Waikiki Bay. **Right:** Waikiki wouldn't be Waikiki without surfboards. It's a wonderfully lively, colorful spot all year round.*

The expression "natural paradise" is a very over-used term. So which qualities does a particular location, or, in our case, beach need to have to qualify as just that? Perhaps it needs to be utterly unspoilt and well removed from all pollution. Virtually empty and edged by lush green vegetation on the one hand and a gently lapping crystal clear sea teeming with marine life on the other. All true. But there also needs to be that special something that quite literally takes your breath away. That's what we're hoping to do in this section and with these beaches. Each one has a quality that will make you say to yourself: "Yes. This is where I want to be. This is where I want to go."

Ada Mascheroni

NATURAL
paradises

HERON ISLAND
QUEENSLAND

Australia is the world's largest island and smallest continent, covering a surface area of 4.7 million square miles with a population density of just one inhabitant per mile. So if you're the kind of traveler that dreams of endless open space and stunning contrasts, this is the vacation destination for you. You'll find a bit of everything in Australia: tropical rain forests, vast deserts, bush, wind-hewn mountains, modern cities, and, of course, the Great Barrier Reef. Fascinating and incredibly different types of landscape abound in every corner of Australia. Along the coast, you'll come across plenty of big cities. Some like Sydney, Brisbane, and Melbourne are ultra modern and dynamic, while others, such as Perth, Victoria, and Adelaide, are more laidback and sedate. Just a couple of hundred miles inland from those very metropolises you'll find yourself surrounded by completely untamed, pristine nature teeming with unique wildlife. We'd recommend you immerse yourself in Australia's unparalleled natural beauty by flying directly to the state of Queensland, where the Great Barrier Reef awaits. This is truly one of the wonders of the world and

NEARBY

One of the most beautiful of the Great Barrier Reef islands is **Brampton Island,** which lies at the very southernmost tip of the Whitsunday chain and is actually a national park. It has subtropical rain forest, deserted bays, and seven stunning beaches all linked by trails offering 69 miles of hiking. Another of the Whitsundays is Hamilton Island, which is ringed with lovely beaches and crystalline waters. It also has a large nature reserve in its interior, and you're guaranteed a pleasant stay. **Lizard Island** is one of the most exclusive islands in the Reef area and is a great place to explore the glorious underwater world of the famous Clam Gardens.

*Above: A pair of butterfly fish, just two of the Great Barrier Reef's countless inhabitants. **Left:** An aerial view of Heron Island. **Opposite:** Shoals of brightly colored fish welcome divers to their underwater world.*

extends for a breathtaking 1,200 miles. However, it is not a single entity as one might think but rather a grouping of thousands of smaller reefs and islands, some coral, others sandy, with plenty of hotels and tourist facilities.

This is the perfect starting point for various excursions to the Great Barrier Reef, which is so incredibly large that it can actually been seen from space. It is home to literally hundreds of different species of coral, 10,000 types of sponge, 1,500 different fish, including giant grouper, shark, ray, black marlin, and even large sea mammals such as the megathere. There are also manta rays and sea turtles, which you can watch either by taking part in an organized dive or comfortably seated in one of the many clear-bottomed boats. You can even decide to put on a mask and flippers and get in amidst them yourself!

Queensland has warm sunny weather 300 days of the year and the water around the Barrier Reef is very pleasant indeed so you'll be wanting to do plenty of diving. The islands with the best tourist facilities are divided into three geographical groupings: Tropical North Islands, Whitesunday, and Southern Reef. You can take either a helicopter or catamaran from Gladstone on the mainland to one of the gems of the Barrier Reef, the legendary Heron Island. This atoll floats in the very center of the reef right at the Tropic of Capricorn level. Its sumptuous coral and turquoise waters are absolutely bewitching. You'll also be able to watch the whales migrating in September, and in November the turtles lay their eggs. Renowned as one of the finest diving sites in the world, Heron Island is the stuff of vacation dreams.

All you need here is a mask and some flippers to dive into the fascinating nature of the Australian reef—even non-experts will be able to feast their eyes on the sublime coral walls towering tens of feet high that are home to millions of creatures of all kinds. Snorkeling along the water's surface or diving with an oxygen tank on your back means you'll get a real up-close-and-personal look at the reefs and some fantastic photographs to take home with you. You'll see angel fish, butterflyfish, surgeon fish, and leather-jackets, all completely unafraid and rather curious about you. And all against a kaleidoscopic backdrop of floating sea fans, coral, and sponges.

Opposite: *The coral in the sea around Heron Island is dazzlingly colorful.* **Above:** *A stretch of the amazing Great Barrier Reef.* **Right:** *A beautiful waterfront resort beckons.*

WINEGLASS BAY

TASMANIA

Wineglass Bay, lapped by the Tasman Sea and located inside Freycinet National Park, is one of the absolute musts for anyone from the northern hemisphere visiting Tasmania. Known to the locals as Tassie, the island is Australia's smallest state and about as big as Ireland. Although culturally quite British, Tasmania abounds with such exotic nature that it is home to the Tasmanian Wilderness World Heritage Area, which has everything from rain forest to jagged impervious coast. Against this dramatic backdrop, Wineglass Bay is surprisingly gentle and almost Mediterranean. A crescent of soft white sand extending a good 1.5 miles, it is one of the jewels in the crown of the 90-year-old Freycinet National Park. The peninsula was once inhabited by the Aborigines and was discovered in the 17th century by the Dutch navigator Abel Tasman.

It lies on the east coast of the island behind pink granite mountains and about half way between the capital, Hobart, to the south and Launceston to the north. To visit Freycinet, base yourself in Coles Bay and organize excursions from there. The legendary beach is only reachable by sea or on foot. If you come by boat, you'll be able to luxuriate in the wonderful tranquility and swim in the lovely blue waters. However, beware of the ocean currents and tides. It is possible to snorkel and dive here as well as take catamaran or kayak trips (good for dolphin spotting). The other way to get to Wineglass Bay is to climb The Hazards. Your route will take about an hour and a half and you'll have breathtaking views over the bay. You'll be surrounded by lush vegetation—the irises, orchids, and banksias (which are famous for attracting the local parrots) flower in spring. You'll also see plenty of other birds, including sea eagles and big Australasian gannets diving for food.

NEARBY

You'll have a great view of the Freycinet Peninsula from Swansea on Great Oyster Bay. Do visit the **Bark Mill Museum**. The mill dates back to 1855 and includes original machinery and other everyday objects from rural life of the time. Also along the east coast you'll find the **Maria Island National Park,** and you can get there by ferry from Triabunna. There are no cars or shops on the island, just paths through the bush and the spectacular **Painted Cliffs** and **Fossil Cliffs**. The wildlife is astonishing, and if you're lucky at all you'll come upon Forester kangaroos and wallabies.

Above: The unspoilt landscape that provides the backdrop to Wineglass Bay. **Right**: A stunning panoramic vista down onto the beach at Wineglass Bay and its gorgeous emerald green sea.

CABBAGE BEACH
NEW PROVIDENCE

Laidback Paradise Island is located just off Nassau, the capital of the Bahamas. The long, narrow Cabbage Beach is located on its northern shore side and is edged by big shady palm trees. Until just a few years ago, people only came here to enjoy a bit of swimming and tanning in peace and quiet. Nowadays, that's all changed and there's a lot more to do, making Cabbage Beach the perfect choice if you want a relaxing vacation with a little fun thrown in. The golf course at the very eastern tip of the beach, for instance, was given a brilliant facelift in 2000—Sean Connery and Michael Jordan are both regular players there. In fact, it hosts the annual Michael Jordan Celebrity Invitational, during which the greens are crammed with celebrities from the worlds of stage, screen, and sports who throng to this truly exclusive corner of the world for the event. Moving west along the beach, you'll see the Marriot Beach Club, the legendary Ocean Club with its gorgeous new wing, the Sunrise Beach Club, the Sheraton, and, sweetest of all, the Atlantis, one of the world's largest hotels complete with pool, beach, water games, aquarium, casino, and restaurants.

You can, if you wish, flee those artificial havens and simply stroll barefoot along the soft sand of Cabbage Beach or take a dip or two in its warm turquoise waters. The Bahamas are a paradise for fishing enthusiasts—you'll find all kinds of fish here, including bonefish. They're fantastic for big game fishing as well. The waters around the islands are teeming with life, a very strong attraction for many visitors. Fishing here is pretty uncomplicated because you can charter a local boat even if you don't have a license.

NEARBY

Nassau, the capital, developed around a natural harbor, which is now regularly crammed with huge cruise ships. Once a refuge of Caribbean pirates, it is a wonderfully colorful and lively town and has a bank for every 500 inhabitants thanks to the Bahamas' relaxed attitude to the provenance of funds held on account there (most accounts are anonymous). The many pretty reminders of the islands' colonial past alternate with fabulous stores, bars, cafés, and restaurants. However, you can't leave without trying the favorite local dish: fresh **conch salad** (dressed with lime), which is sold from stands.

Above: An exclusive resort overlooks the wonderfully clear, clean waters of New Providence Island. **Right**: Three local fishermen show off a huge wahoo caught during a big game fishing trip.

PRAIA DO GUNGA
ALAGOAS

NEARBY

The State of Alagoas has 140 miles of coastline. Its landscape is made even more beautiful by the many vast lagoons crisscrossing it. The **Roteiro** and **Manguaba** lagoons both lie in the area to the north between Praia do Gunga and the state capital, Maceiò. It's well worth stopping off at the international **Praia do Frances**—it's great for both relaxing and water sports, with plenty of bars and restaurants. You'll also find some great local craft shops along the streets leading off the beach. Don't miss the capital, **Macei**ó, which has a wonderful 1950s boardwalk and a series of brilliantly organized beaches between Ponta Verde and Pajucara. The old town center and its colonial architecture are worth a look, too.

Praia do Gunga is said to be one of Brazil's 10 most beautiful beaches, and with good reason, too, as the São Miguel River curves sinuously here through the white sand on its lazy way to the Atlantic Ocean. The area of the beach that overlooks the mouth of the river is protected by a large barrier reef, which means its waters are wonderfully calm. This makes it ideal for swimming, snorkeling, or kayaking. On the other side, however, the waves are big and powerful—much to the delight of the local surfers.

Praia do Gunga is located 20 miles south of Maceió, the capital of the state of Alagoas in the northeast of Brazil. You can get to it by crossing through a private *fazenda* (farm) on an authorized bus. Once you get through the gate you enter a huge forest filled with more than 30,000 palms and hibiscus. It's an utterly enchanted place with the occasional cabin here and there (they are home to indigenous peoples). When you get to the beach, you'll be greeted by fishermen and other locals who've set up small huts serving iced drinks and grilled fish. There are also sun umbrellas and loungers along the shore, but you just have to stroll along the water's edge and stare at the incredibly soft sand, the sea, and imposing palms to forget the rest of the world. You'll also have complete peace and quiet.

If you decide to approach the beach by sea, you can catch a *jangada* (a local type of sailboat) from the little port of Barra di São Miguel, but there are also motor launches and catamarans. The crossing will only take about 20 minutes. One can only imagine the amazement of the first Portuguese conquistadores when they landed centuries ago. If you'd like a view from on high of the beach, head for Mirante Alto da Santana (rent a buggy on the spot) and you'll have the whole of Barra de São Miguel spread out before you. You'll also be able to watch sea and ocean meet from the cliff tops and feast your eyes on the outline of the coast as far as Maceió.

*Above: The beach at Praia do Gunga and its charming huts. **Opposite**: One of the typical colorful motorboats at Praia do Gunga as it waits to pick up a few tourists.*

JHONNY CAY

SAN ANDRÉS

How many times, when you've felt completely overwhelmed by stress and the sheer grind of everyday life, have you told yourself you'll run away to a tropical island? An island embraced by lush vegetation, dusted with powdery soft sand, and lapped by a crystal clear, clean sea. Sometimes, reality can outdo fantasy, and that happens to be the case with San Andrés, one of the many gorgeous atolls dotting the huge expanse of Colombia's oceans. Surrounded by the deep blue waters of the Caribbean, it is the largest island in the archipelago of the same name which also includes Providencia and Catalina. You'll arrive there after a three-quarter-hour flight from Cartagena, around 430 miles away. From the air, San Andrés looks a little like a sea horse, and its 17 square mile surface area is home to 60,000 people, mostly Colombians. There are also plenty of tourists who flock to this stunningly beautiful spot from all over the world, an unspoilt paradise of gleaming white beaches ringed by coconut palms and dense tropical jungle.

The sea and its wonderful coral reef (the world's third largest in size) attract diving enthusiasts who come here to swim with the multicolored fish, manta rays, and sea turtles. Such is the richness and fragility of the local ecosystem around the island that UNESCO declared San Andrés a "Seaflower Biosphere Reserve" in 2000. This allows its flourishing coral reefs to afford protection to rare species of sea turtle and fish who come here during their delicate mating and reproductive seasons. In the past, however, San Andrés often provided the backdrop for bloody battles for supremacy between Europe's leading powers because of its highly strategic location at the very center of the Caribbean. This not only made it important in terms of trade but also a superb hiding place for the band of English pirates led by the legendary Henry Morgan. It is in these very waters that the filibusters lay in wait for the gold-, silver-, and jewel-laden Spanish galleons making their way back from South America to Europe. Today, the wrecks of gallcons sunk during

NEARBY

The town of **San Andrés**, which gives the island its name, is home to most of the holiday facilities and resorts in the area. Inland, however, you'll also find the tiny hamlet of **La Loma**, which has the island's first Baptist church and is worth a visit. Also inland is **La Lagunita**, a small saltwater lake surrounded by thick tropical vegetation—watch out for the crocodiles! The main attractions, however, are the beaches and outlying atolls, including **Acuario**, with its crystal waters and super-fine sand. You won't want to miss **El Hoyo Soplador** either, a seawater geyser on a stony coral beach. If you then move back along the island's west coast you'll eventually get to **La Piscinita**, also known as West View.

Opposite: *San Andrés is renowned for its "sea of seven colors."* **Left:** *The unspoilt loveliness of Jhonny Cay with its exuberant vegetation stretching right down the water's edge.*

those naval battles are one of the main attractions for divers. Don't miss the stretch of sea known as Nirvana in the south of the island. It is the final resting place of the wrecks of the Blue Diamonds and Nicaraguense, which are now guarded only by silent rays, barracuda, and giant groupers. The best way to explore San Andrés is by bike, scooter, or by chartering a boat at the port. You'll only be a 10-minute spin by motorboat from Jhonny Cay, a tiny coral island about 1 mile off the coast. There, lulled by delights of a crystal sea and soft sandy beaches, you can picnic to the soft sounds of reggae music as you sip a good Colombian rum or nibble on a tasty local fish dish. But don't forget to go for a swim, as Jhonny Cay's waters teem with spectacular tropical fish so used to human contact they'll actually eat food directly out of your hand.

Above: A sea turtle gives a ride to two remoras. **Right:** *The heavenly outlying island of Acuario, a short distance from San Andrés.*

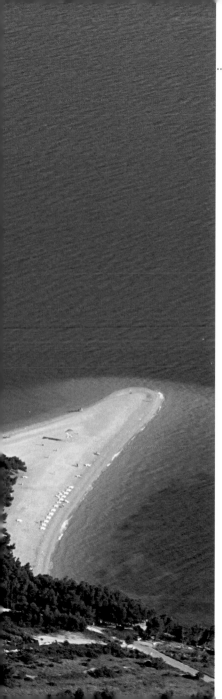

ZLATNI RAT

DALMATIA

Seen from the air, the island of Brac looks incredibly green with a jagged coast and one small point on its western side jutting out towards the island of Hvar directly opposite. As you draw nearer, you see that the point is actually a 2 foot strip of pale beach surrounded by extraordinarily clear blue water that darkens gradually away from the shore. This is Zlatni Rat Beach, "the golden horn," one of the Adriatic's finest corners and probably the only beach in the world that's actually perpendicular to the coast. It is made of shingle, and its tip changes shape and direction with the currents and wind. There are two theories about its formation. The first is that a million years ago, a rock began trapping stones carried by the waves, and over the centuries the "horn" formed. The second, less romantic version was that a large amount of rock was dumped in the sea when the foundations for a winemaking cooperative were being dug in the last century. This created a kind of bank that the wind and waves filled and shaped.

Bol is a lovely little port with stone houses. You can walk from it to Zlatni Rat in about half an hour down the white-stone-paved promenade. Alternatively you can leave your car in the car park and then walk through the pine woods. This is an all-day beach. In the morning, there's a lovely breeze on the calmer side. Then when it gets too hot you can retire to the shade of the pine trees where there are bars, kiosks, and restaurants. There areeven the remains of a Roman villa and swimming pool! The steady afternoon breeze is the perfect excuse to do a bit of windsurfing or kite surfing. Or if you like you can retire to the sheltered side of the beach and just wait for sunset. Immortalized by the world's top photographers and one of the icons of Croatia, Zlatni Rat proves that Europeans don't need to fly for hours to find a Caribbean-style beach: the Mediterranean still has plenty of surprises up its sleeve.

NEARBY

Vidova Gora: at 2,500 feet, this is the highest peak on the Croatian islands and takes its name from the now-ruined Church of Saint Vitus. The summit affords wonderful views, and to get there just follow the Nerezisca road out of Bol. You'll be able to see all the way from Zlatni Rat and the town of Bol, just below you, to the islands of **Hvar**, **Vis**, **Jabuka**, **Peljesac**, and **Korcula**. If it's a very clear day, you'll even be able to catch sight of the Italian coast on the horizon. With its lovely views and stone tables, **Vladimir Nazor's restaurant** serves very good local specialties including raw cured ham, fresh and aged cheeses, lamb, and, of course, the local Bol red wine (a real must).

Opposite: The white sandy Zlatni Rat Beach and, behind it, the dense pine woods. Left: Zlatni Rat Beach is a very unusual shape and runs perpendicular to the coast.

BAYAHIBE
LA ALTAGRACIA

The first explorer to set foot on these islands was Christopher Columbus and it was in this enchanting and undiscovered corner of the world that he established the first European settlement on the American continent, describing it thus: "The most beautiful country that the human eye has ever seen." Columbus was referring, of course, to the island of Hispaniola, today split between the Dominican Republic on one side and Haiti on the other. Over 500 years have passed since those days, but the island retains its magical allure: silky soft white sandy beaches lapped by crystalline waters, dense lush rain forests, and open, friendly people who live their lives to the rhythm of the exuberant merengue.

Bayahibe's beaches lie on the southeastern coast of Hispaniola and really deserve to be explored. The shore is soft white sand dotted with coconut groves and broken up here and there by cliffs and little bays. The interior is carpeted in fertile valleys, irrigated plains, and an incredible variety of ecosystems. The Parque Nacional del Este, home to the largest coastal ecosystem in the entire Caribbean, has all kinds of rare orchids, mahogany forests, and sea birds. Bayahibe is also one of the best places in the Dominican Republic for snorkeling and diving as the waters are warm, clear, and calm, the coral reefs still pristine and teeming with life. The town of Bayahibe was founded by Puerto Rican fishermen in the 19th century, and has retained its original character despite the busy tourist influx. The regional capital is La Romana. The larger tourist resorts are all farther on along the coast. The island just opposite Bayahibe, the Isla Catalina, is also very beautiful and has its own barrier reef and a large variety of tropical fish.

NEARBY

If you head west out of Bayahibe you'll get to **Rio Chavón**, which is a wonderfully wild spot and was used as a location for *Apocalypse Now*. A few miles farther on is **Altos de Chavón**, an artist community set up in the 1970s and built in the style of a 16th-century Mediterranean village. **The Parque Nacional del Este** extends for over 190 square miles to east of Bayahibe. **Saona Island** makes up over 60 square miles of this park and has great beaches and palm groves—perfect for snorkeling and diving. **Casa de Campo**, a tourist resort west of Bayahibe, is a luxury enclave with over 150 exclusive villas.

Above: The exuberant and unspoilt landscape around the Rio Chavón. *Right*: A breathtaking vista of just one stretch of Bayahibe beach.

CORAL BAY
SOUTHERN SINAI

A deserted bay with a rocky, sandy beach gently sloping towards a sea that's home to 1 square mile of unspoilt coral reef with a promontory at either end: Coral Bay is perfect because of those indescribably beautiful coral reefs—which you just have to see in their full glory. It is also one of the most famous beaches in Sharm El Sheik and just a three-hour flight from Italy. The water is always warm enough for swimming (it is slightly cooler in January and February) and it's summer here year-round (autumn, however, is the best time to come). Located in the southern part of the Sinai Peninsula, the story of this famous Egyptian tourist resort is inextricably linked with that of Ernesto Preatoni, the Italian entrepreneur who turned it into a success. In the early 1990s, Naama Bay, the main town on this stretch of coastline, had just a couple of elderly, rather dowdy hotels leftover from the days of the Israeli occupation of Sinai. Nowadays, literally hundreds of hotels line its 25-mile length. Supposedly Preatoni took a helicopter flight over the entire coast and chose this particular stretch of deserted beach because of its unparalleled beauty. Buying up the land from its 60 or so small owners proved complicated as did getting his plans approved and the building started using the local workforce. However, the result of Preatoni's industry is one of the largest tourist resorts in the region. The area's greatest charm still lies in its beach, which is comfortable and well-equipped but also has some lovely quiet, exclusive corners. It also remains the gateway to the area's fascinating underwater world. You can get to the edge of the coral reef from handy floating jetties and then simply dive into the clear, deep waters. All you need is a mask to explore this truly unforgettable underwater paradise.

NEARBY

Take an organized excursion by sea to the **Ras Mohammed National Park**, a protected area at the very southernmost tip of Sinai. The stunning contrast between the desert landscape and the underwater ecosystem is unique: it's home to 200 species of coral, 1,000 types of fish, 40 types of starfish, 25 sea urchins, 100 mollusks, 150 different shell fish and 2 different kinds of sea turtle. Don't miss the atmospheric 6th-century **Monastery of Saint Catherine**, a UNESCO World Heritage Site, built on the site of the Burning Bush.

*Above: Convenient floating jetties bring you right out to the edge of the coral reef. **Right**: Coral Bay's beach is equipped for all kinds of activities, but there are also some wonderfully peaceful spots.*

SALECCIA
CORSICA

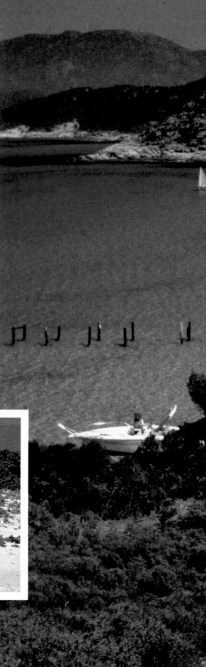

The colors of Saleccia will linger in your memory and in your heart: the pearly white of its sand, the sublime turquoise of the sea, the pale green of the brushy undergrowth, the darker green of the Aleppo pines. Whether you arrive there by boat or on foot, you'll find the long expanse of sand stretching out before you for almost a mile. Located not far from the town of Saint Florent in the Haute Corse department, the beach lies at the foot of Cap Corse. This is a wild, inhospitable, sparsely populated area regularly lashed by the mistral and covered by low-lying arbutus and mastic. Unsurprisingly it's known as the Désert des Agriates. Even getting to Saleccia is tricky. If you don't have a boat of your own to anchor in the bay, you can hitch a ride on one of the tourist boats from the jetty near Plage du Lotu in Saint Florent, but even then you have an hour's hike ahead of you. The only other alternative is to take the State Highway D81 from Saint Florent in the direction of Calvi and then turn off onto a dirt road after a couple of miles or so. After that you'll face an extremely rough 7-mile drive that will challenge even an off-roader. But it will be well worth the effort because right there in the heart of the Mediterranean and on touristy Corsica is a beach as beautiful as any of its Caribbean counterparts. This is a place where the dunes are dotted with sea lilies and the water is so transparent that you can see the ripples on its sandy floor. There are no facilities whatsoever. No kiosks or cafés. You'll spend your day swimming, hiking, and relaxing in the shade of the pines completely surrounded by nature and nothing more. Saleccia was also used to shoot some of the Normandy landing scenes for the film *The Longest Day*.

NEARBY

The port town of **Saint Florent**, now one of Corsica's busiest tourist spots, is around 7 miles away from Saleccia. The 15th-century Genoese **Citadel** and the **Nebbio Cathedral** are its main historical attractions. However, most of the action is at the tourist port, which is thronged with boats in summer and lined with restaurants, bars, and ice cream parlors. It's a big attraction for people who love sailing and vacationers in the evenings after a day at sea. **Calvi** is about 37 miles away, It is home to an attractive and ancient Citadel and what is said to be the house in which Christopher Columbus was born.

*Above: Inland Corsica is sparsely populated and unspoilt so you'll often see cattle grazing freely. **Right:** The beach at Saleccia, which lies at the end of a 7-mile dirt track.*

ANSE DE MAYS
MARIE GALANTE

The beaches of Marie Galante, protected as they are by a coral reef on the Atlantic side and downwind on the Caribbean side, are generally considered the most seductive in the Antilles. However, Anse de Mays near Saint-Louis is the most iconic of them all. From the port at Pointe à Pitre in Guadeloupe, you have 18 miles of sea to cross to get to an area covered in sugar cane plantations and by one of the producers of the finest rum in the Caribbean. Marie Galante is the third largest of the French Antilles in terms of land mass. Almost perfectly round and a little hilly, it is also known as the Island of the Hundred Windmills. Some of these still survive. Apart from the historic Moulin de Bezard, there are a few near the old sugar factories and distilleries. Marie Galante has retained its natural authenticity and wildness.

Hidden by dense palm trees and sea grape, Anse de Mays is the perfect beach for anyone looking for relaxation and plenty of space. As you stroll along this stretch of incredibly fine sandy beach and watch the crystalline waters lap the shore, you'll find your mind slowing down as it is filled with enchantment at the sheer beauty of the sea. The best time to go is between late spring and early summer as at night the sea turtles swim ashore to lay their eggs. You'll know they've been there the following morning by the thousands of little humps of sand along the shore. It takes two months for the young to hatch. Hawksbill, green, and a few very rare leatherback turtles all come here to lay their eggs in a ritual that is repeated every year as each animal returns to its own birthplace. If you continue north towards Gueule Grand Gouffre, the landscape changes dramatically with high rocky cliffs plunging into the sea and an imposing natural arch created by the waves.

NEARBY

On the Atlantic coast, you'll find **Capesterre**, a little town with a fish market restocked with lobster, octopus, and other delights each day by the local fishermen. **Plage de la Feuillère** has the island's best beach facilities, and you can dive there as well as swim with dolphins and turtles. Near upland Pointe de Tali, you'll come upon the rugged **Anse Feuillard**: this is a genuinely unspoilt spot with wonderful nature. Its sandy length is crisscrossed with strips of rock. If you want to find out more about the local history and traditions, go to **Habitation Murat**, an old plantation dating back to the 17th century and now an eco-museum.

*Above: The natural arch of Guele Grand Gouffre. **Opposite:** Anse de Mays, Marie Galante's most heavenly beach.*

SALINE
SAINT-BARTHÉLEMY

There is much more to the irresistibly chic Saint-Barthélemy, better known simply as St. Barts, than the celebrity whirl, yachts, luxury hotels, and designer stores. This little gem in the French Antilles is actually a nature reserve whose flora and fauna are protected. However, man and nature seem to coexist very nicely. It owes its mountainous landscape to its volcanic origins. Valleys run down to the sea creating a jagged coastline with more than 20 very different beaches. The still attractively wild and unspoilt Saline is on the south coast and you can get near to it by car. Then you have to cross through a kind of no-man's land of still pools of water and shriveled trees. It's quite surreal and would be almost dream-like if it weren't for the presence of a few restaurants.

Once you get to Anse du Grand Saline, you have to trek along a rough path but once you emerge from the low Raisin Bord de Mer brush, you'll see Saline beach spread out before you in all its magnificent splendor. An expanse of white sand backed by lush green mountains, it is a refuge for migratory birds. The deep turquoise sea is often rippled by the wind and is wonderfully transparent against the bleached white of the sand. This is an isolated little corner of heaven that epitomizes the very essence of the Caribbean as it was hundreds of years ago. Although nude sun-bathing is officially banned on St. Barts, you will see some here. This is a pristine beach with no facilities whatsoever. Nature reigns supreme. Similar but smaller is Anse de Gouverneur, which lies at the foot of a steep hill and where you'll have complete privacy. Convenient Flamands and Colombier both at the northeastern tip of the island are good choices, too.

NEARBY

If you like fun and a bit of the jet set life, go to **St. Jean beach** near the airport. It's lively and busy, particularly in the peak season when its seafront restaurants are a favorite haunt for international celebrities. This white sandy beach is one of the few set up with sun umbrellas and loungers. It is also a great place for water sports and other nautical activities. Its location makes it ideal for windsurfing, for instance. There are also bars, clubs, boutiques, and the prestigous Eden Rock Hotel.

Above: A villa with its own private jetty on St. Barts. **Right**: The small and very exclusive Anse de Gouverneur on the other side of the Saline bluff.

BANGARAM
LACCADIVES

"Welcome back," declares a strip of white canvas unrolled on the beach at Bangaram. This warm greeting is aimed at guests disembarking on this coral island in the Laccadives for the second time. Having personally welcomed the new arrivals, the general manager explains that there is no hot water, no television, and no air conditioning in any of the bungalows here. The only concessions to the modern age are electric light, ceiling fans, a computer, and a helicopter landing pad. And so even though Laccadives may sound something like Maldives, the atmosphere here is very different. This is a place that people seeking an unspoilt corner come to—Sonia Gandhi is a fan. Lying to the southwest of India, 500 miles off the coast of Malabar, it's an archipelago of 26 little islands that's home to a tolerant Muslim population. You can fly in from Kochi to the island of Agatti from which you'll travel on by fishing boat. Bangaram is surrounded by a 6-mile-long and almost 4-mile-wide coral reef, and its wonderfully silvery beach is home to a resort that epitomizes sophisticated simplicity. By day, you can read on the beach, go for long, relaxing swims, or take a canoe over to a stretch of sand edged by a garden of blue coral. There's even a sunken ship at the bottom of the reef, which you can easily see if you snorkel. Your instructors will take you on excursions as well, to where there are sea caverns, wonderful coral, and brightly colored fish. Bangaram also has fantastic blazing sunsets and its skies are dotted with kites and cormorants. Crabs skitter across its sands. In the evening you'll eat barefoot by candlelight. The menu is delicious: curried and grilled fresh fish, tandoori chicken with mint sauce, fried shrimp. On nights when the moon is full, people gather on the island opposite to watch the sea turtles waddling ashore to lay hundreds of eggs in the sand.

NEARBY

You just can't miss a stop-off in **Kochi**. This is a fascinating seafaring city that controlled the Malabar spice trade for centuries. Time seems to stand still at **Fort Kochi**: the fishing nets still hang on the outliers, the little alleyways in the Jewish quarter with the old synagogue in the background haven't changed in centuries, and there are tiny antique and clothes shops everywhere. Merchants hawk different kinds of rice, mountains of chili peppers, mustard seed, cardamom pods, and coriander for sale. Don't miss touring the town canal by junk.

*Above: The coral reef protects the beach from the waves and makes for delightful catamaran trips. **Right**: The unspoilt vista of the island of Bangaram, where the pace of life is gentle.*

CALA VIOLINA
TUSCANY

Cala Violina is the first genuinely Caribbean-style beach you'll meet moving down from northern Italy. A great part of its charm lies in the fact that it can only be reached on foot by trekking through the primordial Maremma, south of Follonica and north of Punta Ala, or more specifically, the 21,000-acre Bandite di Scarlino Nature Reserve, a huge expanse of open countryside, impenetrable Mediterranean brush and foliage, parasol pines, ancient watchtowers, and turquoise waters. There is a path leading to this area of virgin coastline and you have a choice of walking, mountain biking, or horse riding down to it. If you leave from the newly built Marina di Scarlino near Puntone, you'll soon find yourself surrounded by lush green countryside with flashes of blue water here and there. You'll catch sudden glimpses of the Bay of Follonica, the Piombino promontory, the islands of Elba, Cerboli, Montecristo, and, on a clear day, Corsica. The dark shady woods give way to rocky coves of the likes of Cala Francese and Cala Martina, where you'll see a stone in the sea and a monument dedicated to Garibaldi, who escaped here in 1849. After around 2.5 miles, you'll get to Cala Violina. Nestling between two bluffs, its transparent waters glitter and gleam in the sunshine and its spectacular colors dazzle the eyes. At dusk, the sun seems to sink into the sea itself. The sea floor is sandy with expanses of posidonia seaweed and sandstone peeking through. Unsurprisingly, you'll often find heaps of seaweed washed upon the shore: posidonia helps prevent erosion, oxygenates the water, and is a major indicator of the health of the local environment. The quartzite sand isn't incredibly white, but it is superbly fine and powdery. In fact, when you walk on it barefoot, it produces a violin-like sound—hence the name Cala Violina.

NEARBY

A very pretty fortified village perched on the side of a lush green hill, **Scarlino** has to be one of Maremma's best-kept secrets. Its 600 inhabitants live on the 800 ft. high **Monte d'Alma**. The scene is dominated by the rock, the archaeological park, and various ruins. **Piazzale della Stella** affords very pleasant views of the old port, churches, and various high-ranking palazzos, including the 13th-century Town Hall. All in all, Scarlino is a beautiful town architecturally and includes such treasures as the **Madonna degli Angeli**, the **church of San Donato**, and the **Augustinian monastery**.

*Above: The islet of Cerboli can be seen from the trail leading to Cala Violina. **Right**: Despite being quite difficult to get to, Cala Violina is always busy in the summer months.*

PISCINAS
SARDINIA

s you round the last treacherous bend overlooking the estuary of the Rio Piscinas, you'll catch your first glimpse of soft, powdery dunes as welcoming as a warm embrace. Ochre sand stretches as far as the eye can see. A surreal silence broken only by the regular whoosh of the tide. There is just one building on this four-mile beach, a tiny sliver of the Sahara that melts into the sea and one of the most unspoilt and significant ecosystems in the entire Mediterranean. This is probably the only section of Sardinia's coastline that hasn't changed over the last few hundred years. Towering up to 160 feet, the sand dunes at Piscinas stretch back inland with splashes of Mediterranean brush here and there, humble but stubborn as it goes about its colonizing business. Noisy bee-eaters flit about from scented mastic trees to asphodel, fragile ephedra, soldanella, sea lilies, and juniper bushes wizened by the wind. The morning sand is crisscrossed with ephemeral signs of the lives of industrious beetles, lazy colubers, timid wild rabbits, and wary foxes. The silky sand will also be dotted with the delicate tracks of the little Sardinian deer, probably the most precious of all the inhabitants of the Piscinas dunes (a 2-square-mile nature reserve) and the craggy Monte Arcuentu. An intriguing mineral-rich universe and a UNESCO World Heritage site survives behind this odd coastal landscape. You can still feel the exhaustion in the air at the extraction plant at Ingurtosu, the treatment plant at Naracauli, and the deserted village of Montevecchio, a group of homes that once housed the miners and other workers. A perfect microcosm that brings alive the ghosts of a tough but wealthy past. They had everything: a post office, church, hospital, newspaper kiosk and a grocery store, cinema, dance hall, hotel, and an elegant Art Nouveau home for the mine manager, which has now been turned into a museum. An abandoned place but one that still lives on in a way. An emotional experience indeed.

NEARBY

Surrounded by sand, the **Hotel Le Dune** is a former 19th-century mine warehouse that's been elegantly renovated by the son of the last manager of the Igurtosu mine. This very unusual hotel is actually a national monument but looks a little like a fortress. It is made up of three buildings that share a central courtyard and a square that opens onto the sea. The central building was once stabling for the horses used to pull the wagons to the mine and now houses 10 bedrooms and a courtyard showcasing archaeological items retrieved from the sea around Piscinas.

*Above: Evidence of the area's mining heritage. **Opposite:** The ochre landscape of Piscinas with dunes and brush stretching as far as the eye can see.*

SPIAGGIA ROSA

SARDINIA

Just off the northeast of Sardinia, a short distance from Corsica, is a group of 7 large islands and several smaller islets making up the La Maddalena Archipelago. This has always been a military area because of its strategic location but is actually a place of unique natural beauty thanks the poignant scents of its Mediterranean brush, jagged granite rock, and an incredibly clear sea thanks to the strong currents from the Bocche di Bonifacio. The archipelago has many enchanting and varied beaches dotting its innumerable bays. However, don't miss Cala di Roto. Located on the southeastern side of the island of Budelli, it is more commonly known as Spiaggia Rosa or Pink Beach because of the unusual pinky color of its very fine powdery sand, which itself is the result of the miraculous work of a protozoa called *Miniacina miniacea*. This tiny microorganism grows on the posidonia seaweed in the area and gets washed ashore by the tide.

To safeguard this incredibly fragile little corner of heaven on earth, the Italian government not only declared Budelli a protected marine area but also prohibited landing by boat. In certain areas, in fact, neither foot traffic nor swimming are allowed at all. Like a masterpiece in a museum, you can look but you can't touch: along the pristine crescent of beach, there's a walkway built using salvaged wood by the island's only resident, Mauro Morandi, about 60 feet from the actual shore. Morandi lives in a former military barracks. In winter, he has a hermit-like existence, but in summer, he has plenty of company from friends and tourists alike. The barracks is also the ideal place from which to ensure that not as much as a grain of sand is taken away as a souvenir. He says that the easterly wind does erode the beach, then by some miracle the westerly ones add to it. Spiaggia Rosa was immortalized in a long sequence in Michelangelo Antonioni's 1960s movie *Red Desert* and retains the same charm today.

NEARBY

Apart from the 6 other large islands (**La Maddalena, Caprera, Santo Stefano, Spargi, Razzoli,** and **Santa Maria**), the clean windy seas around Budelli are dotted with many other islets: **Cappuccini, Piana, Barrettini, Bisce, Porco, Soffi, Mortorio, Monaci, Pecora, Camere,** and **Nibani**. All names that hark back to times long past. If you have a boat, do sail out as far as **Spargi**. Tie up at the old military dock in Cala Corsara and have a good walk around. Its waters are an enchanting emerald green. Another must is **Razzoli,** which has great cliffs and a lighthouse. The **Porto della Madonna**, the channel between the islands, is well worth exploring, with its breathtaking coves and bays.

Opposite: Spiaggia Rosa (Pink Beach) owes its name to its unusual color. **Left:** *There is a huge variety of wildflowers to be found in the vegetation edging Spiaggia Rosa.*

DIANI BEACH

COAST

KENYA

Kikoys flapping like bright flags in the wind, a turquoise sea, gleaming white sand. Three camels appear over the horizon while a cook in a mushroom hat strolls along the beach and another man with a basket scans his surroundings for seashells. The shoreline at Diani Beach affords a string of strong, contrasting images that flash before you and go straight to the heart. There's the bright scarlet of a painting for sale on the beach, the vivid green of the baobabs and the coconut palms, the deep blue of the Indian Ocean ruffled by the trade winds. This is a genuinely enchanted strip of water, sand, foliage, and sky. Diani Beach lies on the Kenyan coast to the south of Mombasa and is a vibrant tropical paradise that stretches for 15 miles. You have to take a ferry to get here, but the journey is only about 10 minutes. World renowned for its incredibly white, powdery sand, Diani really is a paradise for divers and snorkelers. It looks like it belongs in the Maldives because of that fine, fine sand, crystal clear sea, and incredibly colorful and rich marine life. However, the colors of its coral reef are absolutely unique as it's alive with madrepore coral, sea anemones, and tropical fish. Diani is the perfect place for snorkeling and diving. On low-tide days, the coral reef is transformed into endless little saltwater aquariums teeming with miniscule fish and other marine life. This is very much a tourist haven so Diani is lined with resorts and bungalows all in the local Swahili style with a few Arabic influences. Their intricate carved wood and bright fabric drapes feel like an instinctive hymn of praise to nature and freedom.

The local people are exceptionally friendly and willing to chat. If you go to Diani, you'll probably want to return again and again. Many Europeans have actually settled here and now work in the local hotel industry. "It's a healthy lifestyle," they invariably report. "You're always in contact with Africa's unspoilt nature and that really does bring out the creativity

NEARBY

The **Shimba Hills National Reserve** is just a half-hour's drive from Diani. As your jeep crashes through the dense undergrowth and brush, wonderful fragrances and scents will surround you. You'll hear the rustle of a francolin as it swoops away and then see the flash of a gazelle in full flight. The leisurely pace of a herd of elephants will slow you down and the stony stares of absolutely immobile buffalo stop you in your tracks. You'll start your day at the Reserve with a scarlet dawn and end it as the sky turns a dusky indigo at sunset. You'll see all the colors of the rainbow on a single day and your heart will beat to the rhythm of the drums filling the night air.

Opposite: A local man selling shells on Diani Beach. Left: One of the bungalows in a resort nestling in the dense tropical vegetation edging the shore at Diani Beach.

that's inside us all." Because of its luxurious connotations, Diani Beach is often called one of the world's most beautiful beaches. And it is a genuinely enchanting spot. Whether you just lay there in the sun or stroll along the shore, you will have the privilege of watching a unique spectacle unfold before you each and every day. Your surroundings are dominated by the green of its vegetation and the white of its sand, making them absolutely unique.

Above: Colorful sarongs and kikoys for sale on the beach. **Right:** *If you're feeling adventurous, try a camel ride along the shore at Diani Beach.*

GRANDE ANSE DES SALINES
SAINTE-ANNE

NEARBY

One area of considerable interest to nature lovers will be **Savane des Pétrifications**—there's a trail leading directly to it from Les Salines beach. This is an ancient former swamp with a lunar landscape: the ground is dry and barren and scattered with multicolored jasper and huge hunks of silica. Cacti, prickly pear, and gnarled silk cotton trees struggle along in between. **Sainte-Anne** is also worth a visit—it's the home of Caribbean ceramics. Now a lively tourist town, its history is linked with that of the Napoleonic General Bertrand and the war with the English. Its flower-bedecked, colorful wooden houses, the church of Sainte-Anne, and the chapel of Notre Dame de la Salette lend it a unique coastal charm.

The exotic island of Martinique in the Lesser Antilles is edged by white sandy shores broken up at regular intervals by exotic volcanic rock formations. At its very southernmost tip lies Grande Anse des Salines, whose splendidly Caribbean beach remains a genuine natural paradise despite being an allure for tourists and locals alike. Many would say, in fact, that it is the most idyllic beach in all the Antilles, and while that claim may be open to debate, there is no doubt it is the finest on Martinique and a must-see that never fails to live up to expectations.

Les Salines is basically the iconic Caribbean beach par excellence. It literally is postcard picture beautiful: an enormous and perfect crescent of soft powdery sand that takes on a wonderful gilded beauty in the warm glow of sunset. It is edged by balmy, shady *cocotiers* (coconut palms) and lapped by crystalline waters of deep turquoise-blue waters. Jutting out of these waters are a large bluff of calcareous rock known as the *Table du Diable* (Devil's Table, Satan's cohorts are said to gather!) and the little island of Cabrit. The latter is very popular with divers as its waters conceal the remains of a sunken ship, which is fun to explore. These are the two southernmost points of Martinique. Lying around 3 miles from the town of Sainte-Anne, the beach, which takes its name from L'Etang des Salines, a large saltwater lake nearby, has another interesting feature: a vast green area that belongs to the state-owned forest along the shore. Its sumptuous plant life includes cacti and *raisiniers bord de mer*, shrubs with white flowers that bear fruit resembling grapes. However, please do be aware of the *mancenilliers* (manchineel trees)—they are poisonous to humans. In fact, their small green apple-like fruit produce a milky substance that will burn your skin. It is thus highly inadvisable to sit under them. You'll see that most are marked with red stripes on their trunks to warn visitors.

Above: The intense colors of a blazing sunset at Plage des Salines. **Opposite:** *The dense vegetation and transparent sea that edge the Plage des Salines.*

BELLE MARE

FLACQ

A mosaic of causarinas and filaos, labyrinths of palm and sugar plantations, crescent beaches and then, spreading out before you, the Indian Ocean itself. Mauritius is an ylang-ylang and vetiver-scented paradise. The eastern part of the island is clothed by miles of beach, unfurling like ribbons, one after another, along its coastline. Just outside the little village of Trou d'Eau Douce in the district of Flacq, in fact, you'll come upon the beach of Belle Mare, widely considered one of the most idyllic on the entire island of Mauritius. It really does have it all: its white sandiness is in spectacular contrast to the stunning greens of the interior and the glittering turquoise and aquamarine of the waves. A tropical paradise stretching 4 long miles, Belle Mare beach is a place to savor at your leisure. Dig your toes into its talc-soft sand as you gaze out at the spectacular Ile aux Cerfs, a private island with its own 18-hole golf course and perfect little coves for diving.

Belle Mare is also famous for its lagoon—just the place for small boats. And for its breathtakingly intricate coral reef: some areas are a long way from the beach, while others are just about 300 yards from the shore. This is a place with a real personality. Its ocean depths are home to veritable forests of marine vegetation with wonderful underwater canyons teeming with a variety of fish of every imaginable size, shape, and color. If you're really lucky you might happen upon the diamond fish, the world's smallest vertebrate, whale shark, carangids, barracuda, wahoos, several different species of sea turtles, and Madagascar fish eagles.

Belle Mare is also a great base for a host of dive sites of various kinds and depths: from the Valley of the Sea Fans, the Japanese Garden via the Castle (a coral labyrinth), and La Passe du Puits, a gorgeous reef and easily one of the most spectacular on the east coast of Mauritius.

NEARBY

Not far from Belle Mare, there's the town of **Flacq**, which is home to Mauritius' largest and most colorful outdoor market. It takes place not far from the courthouse and is a great sight to see a lot without actually having to go very far. The colors, flavors, and species have a wonderful Indian influence to them. **Poste de Flacq** has one of Hinduism's most famous temples. Another great beach on the coast is at **Trou d'Eau Douce,** while a 10-minute boat ride will bring you to the private island of **Ile aux Cerfs**. We'd also recommend a drive inland from Belle Mare where the gently rolling mountains are a patchwork of sugar cane plantations.

Opposite: A luxury hotel near Belle Mare on the island of Mauritius. **Left:** *The wonderful Belle Mare beach hasn't lost any of its tropical personality despite having facilities.*

LE MORNE
LE MORNE BRABANT

NEARBY

Just a 15-minute drive north of the Le Morne Brabant Peninsula are the spectacular forests of the **Black River Gorges National Park**, a wild, dense expanse of trees, waterfalls, valleys, and streams that provides a habitat for over 300 species of flowering plant. You can drive through it by automobile or bus or, better still, hike along the numerous trails with a guide. **Chamarel** is also worth a visit—the waterfall there tumbles a breathtaking 300 or so feet. Don't miss **Les Terres de Couleur** either, a kaleidoscope of ochre, red, and yellow earth caused by rapidly cooling volcanic rocks. In the sunlight, the area becomes a superlative palette of colors and a genuine feast for the eyes.

A lush garden floating serenely a little to the north of the Tropic of Capricorn, Mauritius exudes a unique energy. It's an energy that comes from the population itself, for Mauritius is a genuine melting pot of ethnicities, customs, religions, and traditions. You can feel its vitality in the villages, its music and dance, its festivals, and, most of all, on the 4-mile-long strip of white sandy beach that winds its way around the Le Morne Brabant peninsula, on the southwestern side of the island. Here the pale, powdery sand is lapped by a turquoise sea and protected by a coral reef so gorgeous it looks and feels like the inside of a giant shell. The murmur of the sea tells the tale of waves breaking on far-off shores, adventures past and future dreams consigned to the horizon. Standing guard over this gentle universe of color and sound is the massive Le Morne Brabant, an imposing 1,780-foot-high spur of rock whose caves provided the perfect hiding place for runaway plantation slaves in the dark days of the 19th century. Legend has it that one day in 1835, the escapees saw a group of soldiers approaching and rather than be taken back to a life of servitude on the plantations, threw themselves off the side of the mountain. Tragically, the soldiers were coming only to bring them the good news that slavery had been abolished. This earned the mountain the new name of Le Morne, "The Mourner."

It is now a UNESCO World Heritage Site and continues to exude its wonderful sense of power and energy. The colors are particularly vivid in this little corner of paradise. The light is clear and the sounds deep and absolutely true. Or perhaps it's just that our senses become so much more receptive. Visitors can swim with dolphins each morning or explore colorful coral reefs around the mushroom-shaped Benitier Rock. As the sun goes down, the stars come out: millions of far-off lights twinkling in the night sky like a shower of gold. You'll clearly see the Southern Cross, which looks like an eagle poised over the horizon. A fantastic way to ease into the sweet Mauritian night.

*Above: Benitier Rock off the beach at Le Morne. **Right**: The beach at the foot of the brooding Le Morne Brabant massif.*

NGAPALI BEACH
RAKHINE

Widely renowned as Myanmar's (formerly Burma) most idyllic beach and once completely isolated and secret, Ngapali Beach, on the southwest coast of the remote state of Arakan (Rakhine) in the Indian Ocean, is now easily reached from Yangon, thanks to the nearby airport in the city of Thandwe, once known as Sandoway by the English.

The heart of the white sandy beach stretches a good 4 miles under a shady line of coconut palms and causarina. A dozen or so small hotels have attracted tourists to the beach which, local legend has it, was named in honor of the city of Naples. The luxury Sandoway Resort, designed by the renowned architect Alberto Peyrè in the local Asian style, has captured the attention of well-heeled international travelers thanks to its superb design and Italian hospitality. That said, tourism has done little to change the very traditional way of local life—most people continue to make their living by fishing and rice-growing inland. Ngapali Beach is a wonderfully sunny, good-humored place and evokes the same kind of old-fashioned nostalgia as a Rudyard Kipling tale. Kids playing in the simple little local fishing villages, monks begging for alms, the slow rhythm of carts hauled by buffalos and laden with nets and all kinds of goods, lines of men and women making their way to the market with baskets of fish balanced gracefully on their heads. Ngapali has it all. However, the whole day centers around the departure and the return of the traditional fishing boats. The catch is unloaded onto the beach each evening and will include everything from big fish such as tuna, shark, groupers of various kinds, and carangid as well as smaller ones such as sardines and shrimp.

Pearl oysters were once fished for and cultivated on Pearl Island. This is a lovely spot ringed by a ribbon of wonderful sand that runs directly onto Ngapali at low tide and today is an absolute favorite of any tourist lucky enough to visit it.

NEARBY

Don't forget to pay a visit to the fishing village of **Singaung** at the mouth of the river Thandwe, around 15 miles north of Ngapali. After doing their fishing in the open sea, the boats take refuge in the estuary, which is dotted with little coves hidden in the mangrove swamps. The main part of the village Singaung gives a wonderful insight into everyday maritime life in these parts. It zigzags along an ochre beach with huts made of rattan and woven palm leaves. The nets and freshly caught fish are unloaded onto floating jetties. Other huts and small communities of fishing folk are hidden away in innumerable inlets. The best way to visit Singaung is by sea—just charter a motorboat from Ngapali.

*Above: The unmistakably exotic atmosphere of Ngapali Beach. **Opposite:** Local people going about their everyday life at sunset on the beach.*

AITUTAKI
COOK ISLANDS

A stunningly white beach, a palette in which turquoise and sky blue have been cleverly mixed by the artist. A trip to the fabulous Cook Islands is a once-in-a-lifetime experience that everyone should try, because the light will enter your mind and capture your soul. The Cook archipelago consists of 15 small islands that have been scattered over 2 million square miles of ocean, ideally placed at the center of the Polynesian Triangle in the South Pacific. The largest island is Rarotonga (42 square miles), the smallest is Suwarrow (0.25 square miles). The most extraordinary is Aitutaki, a terrestrial paradise: its lagoon is one of the most enchanting places on earth. Silence reigns supreme in this harmonious site where even the waves seem to make no sound as they lap against the shore. The wind rustles gently in the trees and fish dart curiously between your feet. The scenery is utterly still, but too bursting with wonderful color. Here and there you'll see *marae*, ancient places of worship. Sometimes you will come across the Maori, the original inhabitants. They are cheerful and hospitable, but never intrusive. They are amazing dancers, music is in their blood, and they know how to transmit this passion to tourists during evenings on the beach, in which the stars brighten up the sky. The dancing and the singing are in honor of Tangaroa, the god of fertility and of the sea. Appetites are easily satisfied on this island: the typical delicate dishes include raw fish in coconut sauce (*ika mata*), the fruit of the trees stuffed into bread (*anga kuru akaki ia*), and bread pudding (*poke*). As tourists leave, not only do they take with them the indelible memory of a lost Eden, they can also acquire colorful arts and crafts products: the traditional axes with stone blades and the notched wooden handles, fans, belts, baskets, feather hoods, and wooden chairs.

NEARBY

Don't miss the atoll of **Suwarrow**, where New Zealand writer Tom Neale took refuge from modern civilization. He stayed there 11 years during which time he wrote the classic book *An Island to Oneself*. Another piece of paradise is the island of **Atiu**, where you can admire *makatea*, rings of fossilized coral. **Wigmore's Waterfall**, which drops into a natural turquoise blue and emerald green pool, is not to be missed. Last but not least, the marvels of nature in the town of Avrua: the **Seven-in-One Coconut Tree**, seven trees that have grown to make a perfect circle. At Avra you can also visit the **Cicc Church**, which dates back to 1853, and the **Museum Society**, with its objects in wicker-made artifacts, musical instruments, and numerous photographs of a bygone age.

Opposite: An enchanted corner of the island of Aitutaki. Left: The dazzlingly white beach runs along the island's perimeter with palm groves on one side and clear blue sea on the other.

PONELOYA
LEÓN

One of Central America's most famous poets, Ruben Dario, used to sunbathe on this long black sandy beach. A century later, it retains the same unspoilt charm. In fact, Poneloya's lengthy shore is virtually deserted most of the year and really only gets crowded with vacationers for a few weekends. For the rest of the time, silence reigns supreme and is broken only by the crashing of the Pacific waves over which pelicans and cormorants swoop. In August and September, sea turtles come to the beach to lay their eggs in the sand. When the eggs hatch, there is a flood of baby turtles trying to scurry down to the sea without being picked off by crabs, birds, and dogs. The sea around here is pretty rough with long ocean waves perfect for surfing. Strong currents, however, make swimming dangerous, particularly for the inexperienced. You're far better off to just take a paddle or two in the waves at the water's edge after a long relaxing stroll—there's plenty of room as the beach is 6 miles of unending sand, interrupted only here and there by the occasional *peñon* of rock. Overlooking the shore are vacation homes with flower-filled balconies, and quaint restaurants offering delicious grilled fish flavored with garlic and washed down with beer or, better still, good Nicaraguan rum.

You might end your stroll in the quiet fishing bay of Las Peñitas, which is separated from Poneloya by a small rocky promontory. In the distance, you'll see the island of Juan Venado, a protected area reachable only by boat and a haven for thousands of sea birds. However, the most stunning memories you'll take away with you are the sunsets, which set the sky blazing with a thousand colors.

NEARBY

Twelve miles from Poneloya is **León**, a colonial town razed to the ground by pirates in 1685. However, it still has its cathedral, which was enlarged in 1860, making it the largest in Central America. It is also the burial place of Ruben Dario and other Nicaraguan greats. Don't forget to visit the **Museum of Legends and Traditions**, the **Ruben Dario Museum**, and the ruins of **León Viejo** which was abandoned because of volcanic eruptions and has been declared a UNESCO World Heritage Site. Located near Lake Managua, it affords beautiful views of the **Momotombo volcano**.

*Above: Poneloya beach is linked to the town of León by convenient shuttle bus service. **Right:** The sandy beach at Poneloya and the long ocean waves that break along it.*

MANIHI
TUAMOTU ISLANDS

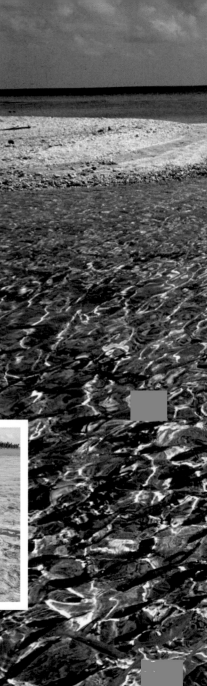

Manihi is something of a black pearl itself. The Polynesian atoll is part of the Tuamoto Islands and is located 325 miles from Tahiti and to the northeast of Rangiroa. Black pearl production is in fact the main source of income for its inhabitants and the coveted pearls adorn the slender necks of many of the islands' graceful female inhabitants. Manihi is an elongated oval-shaped atoll whose central lagoon is dotted with tiny islands. Its underwater gardens are lush with coral of all kinds and an endless variety of tropical fish including Napoleon fish and majestic rays. There is just one navigable channel, Passe Tairapa, linking the lagoon to the open sea. Manihi is the world's leading pearl producer and was the first island anywhere in the world to have pearl farms, which were first set up in the 1960s. The main industries here are trade, tourism, and fishing. The largest villages are Paeua and Turipaoa, in the southwest. At the time of the 2002 census, the island had a population of 789 inhabitants but that number has probably fallen to under 500 now. The first Europeans to reach here are said to have been the Dutch explorers Jacob Le Maire and Willem Schouten, who landed on these beaches and named the atoll Waterland Island during their Pacific voyage of 1615–16. The Tuamotu Islands to which Manihi belongs are a collection of 85 atolls where land and sea meet, and where 852 rings made up entirely of coral and madrepore turn the dreams of divers into glorious reality. Despite being so remote from the rest of the world, Tuamotu has all the modern comforts, conveniences, and communications systems. The local electricity is produced by solar power, and rain water is collected in tanks.

NEARBY

Do explore the fantastic underwater "museums" in these waters: **Pass Tombant, Circo**, the **Falile,** and **Tairapa**. You can't afford to miss a tour of the pearl farms and the ruins of the *marae* (ancient sacred sites) dotted around the rim of the coral reef. **Rangiroa, Tikehao,** and **Fakarava** are all worth the trip also. They and the other inhabited islands (around 30) have tourist accommodations of all kinds from luxury resorts to small guesthouses. The **Manihi Pearl Beach Resort** runs the **Manihi Blue Nui**, a dive center that organizes courses and offers guided dives—the nighttime ones are exceptionally good.

Above: Small black fin sharks sometimes manage to make it over the coral reef and get in quite close to the shore.
Right: A shoal of fish glitters brilliantly just under the surface of the water.

PRAIA POMBAS
SÃO TOMÉ

A t dawn on December 21, 1451, the Portuguese navigator and explorer Pedro de Escobar first set foot on what is now known as Praia Pombas.

It was the Feast of Saint Thomas, *São Tomé* in Portuguese, and, of course, Escobar quickly named his new discovery in the saint's honor. The long, wide Praia Pombas, edged by gentle coconut palms, is home to a nesting area for sea turtles, five different species of which come here between October and February each year to lay their eggs in the sand. São Tomé is one of the islands off the coast of Equatorial Guinea in Central Africa and is probably one of a few places left in the world that makes one feel more a genuine traveler than a tourist. The local population is descended from the Bantu (an ancient sub-Saharan African people), its vegetation is dense and impenetrable, its beaches pristine. You can still visit the local coffee and cocoa plantations, and watch the local fishermen come home at night in their pirogues. There are no brochures to tell you where to go. This is an entirely undiscovered island: the roads, which were built by the Portuguese and maintained by them until the island gained independence in 1975, are in a pretty poor state. Unfortunately, when the Portuguese left, so did their money and the government simply hasn't been able to pay for their upkeep. Europeans stopped investing in the country after independence and priority has been given to other sectors like health and education.

You won't have to go very far on São Tomé to find your first spellbinding views: this tiny island is Africa in miniature. Its landscape is arid to the north with baobabs running all the way down to the shore in the lovely inlet of Lake Azul, in stark contrast with the luxuriant vegetation that thickens most of its surface. A few miles away on the tiny island of Das Cabras, you'll come upon a genuinely Mediterranean-looking rock, the famous "tooth" of Cão Grande, a bizarre 1,900-foot-tall shard of jutting rock that can be seen from the abandoned lighthouse.

NEARBY

Exploring the charming island of **São Tomé** will involve trekking its many gorgeous beaches. You'll also have to immerse yourself in its agrarian culture by visiting its cocoa and coffee plantations (some of the best cocoa beans in the world come from here). The Portuguese left behind them a series of *rochas*, small impendent agricultural communities that include not only homes for the owners but also for the farm workers, schools, and hospitals. In the small capital of São Tomé on the northeast coast, the architecture is typical Portuguese colonial fare with lots of pastel ochre and yellows. You can also travel out from here to **Principe**, a smaller town whose character is just as wild and exotic.

Above: The completely deserted beach at Praia Pombas. ***Opposite:*** *The imposing Cão Grande juts into the night sky on the island of São Tomé.*

There are places that will always stay in our hearts on account of their colors, their inhabitants, their wildlife, and their aromas. One such is the island of Zanzibar, which is infused with scents that are sweet, spicy, intense, and unforgettable. Zanzibar is not so much a physical location as a state of mind, a place that many people have heard of, without actually being able to pinpoint it on a map.

Its name comes from "zandj barr," which means "land of the black people," the term that Arab and Persian traders used to indicate the East African coast, which they often visited. Indeed, this archipelago in the Indian Ocean, which consists of two main islands, Unguja and Pemba, and a host of smaller ones, has been an important trading post since time immemorial. There were frequent battles for supremacy, in which African, Persian, and Arab dynasties took it in turns.

In the 19th century Seyyid Said, the governor of Oman, "promoted" Zanzibar from a sultanate to the capital of the entire region. Zanzibar Town, which was the product of the economic

NEARBY

Zanzibar Town, the capital of the island, is a city rich in both culture and architecture. The most beautiful and interesting part of the island of Unguja is undoubtedly **Stone Town**, the old city, which is about 25–28 miles from the beach of Pwani Mchangani. This was the birthplace of Freddie Mercury, the legendary lead singer of Queen. Of particular interest are the huge inlaid wooden gates of the buildings which, in the past, determined the social status of the owner. In architectural terms, the spectacular **House of Wonder**, which was built in 1883, the **Arab Fort**, and the **Peace Memorial Museum** are all worth a visit. And everywhere in Stone Town you will find street traders who sell sarongs, *tinga tinga*—typical oil paintings—and local culinary specialties.

Above: A woman gathers algae on the beach. **Left**: *The colors of the beach at Muyuni.* **Opposite**: *Fishermen on their way to work by bike on the beach at Pwani Mchangani.*

boom of that century, quickly became the most important city in East Africa. Zanzibar became an independent state in 1963 and, the following year, a republic. 1964 also saw the birth of the United Republic of Tanzania, a name that was created from the first three letters of the two relevant countries, Tanganika and Zanzibar.

Of the island's many attractions particular attention should be paid to the beach at Pwani Mchangani. The surroundings are impressive, consisting of spice plantations and their female workers. Here the spices are decidedly different from the ones that we are used to in the West. Without our sense of taste and smell it would be impossible to recognize the strange fruit with a bright cover: nutmeg. Nor would we know that a twisting creeper was the source of black pepper. The most curious thing that you can witness is the production of soap suds, which are obtained by rubbing small green berries in your hands. It's a soap which, they assure us, can clean even the toughest dirt!

In the shallow waters that lap against the beaches of Pwani Mchangani, the women have invented a new profession: the cultivation of algae. This is done by stretching ropes between wooden poles placed at regular intervals in the sand. Little pieces of algae are attached and within two weeks these more than double in size, thereby creating a living necklace.

The low tide indicates the moment for harvesting. The algae are bunched in sheafs and then separated for their quality and left to dry for a few days before being placed in sacks. They will then be sold on both the foreign and national markets for culinary, cosmetic, and medicinal purposes. Today the algae trade is an important part of the economy.

The beach at Pwani Mchangani is very beautiful. It's a large space which opens towards the horizon; the white sand and the superb view of the coral reef make it the perfect location for anyone seeking complete relaxation. A combination of the dhow—the typical Arab lateen sailboats, which for centuries sailed the Indian Ocean—and the tides mean that the beaches at Pwani Mchangani are the finest in Zanzibar.

Opposite: A dhow, the typical lateen sailboat. *Above:* Coral floating in the water at low tide. *Right:* Two Masai walking along the shore.

FRANCISQUI
LOS ROQUES

L os Roques is an archipelago of around 50 coral islands and more than 250 sandy atolls. They lie around 100 miles north of the Venezuelan capital of Caracas and are lapped by the Caribbean. The main island, El Gran Roque, is the only one that's inhabited and has a population of around 1,500, sandy little roads, and a host of *posadas*, tourist accommodation in converted fishermen's homes. All of the other islands can be reached by boat but you can't stay overnight—one feature that makes this archipelago particularly charming and gives it a timeless appeal. In 1972, the Los Roques Islands were made into a national park to protect the incredible biodiversity of the marine species living in their waters, their coral reefs, and extraordinary wildlife (there are 92 species of bird alone). At the very northern end of the part is Francisqui, one of the many little islands in the chain and the beach of the same name. Francisqui has a surface area of around 6 square miles and it takes about a quarter of an hour to get there by boat. It's a truly magical spot whose blindingly white beach provides a startling contrast with the blues and greens of the sea. They range from a deep cobalt in deeper water to turquoise and then sky blue as you draw near to the shore, with a pinkish hue here and there. Paddling and snorkeling take on a whole new adventurous meaning as you'll be surrounded by stunningly colorful fish going about their business in the shallows or near the coral reefs. Take a barefoot stroll around the island. Head east and then inland where you'll come up on coral rock gardens and a ghostly saltwater lake. After eating the light meal prepared by the owner of your *posada*, and having spent a day in a place quite literally out of this world, your boat will return to ferry you back to El Gran Roque. That way you can get yourself organized for another island the next day.

NEARBY

If you find yourself in this truly fantastic corner of the world, you simply have to visit **Dos Mosquises**. Apart from a small private airstrip, it also has a sea turtle sanctuary. For the price of a few dollars you can tour the facility and your money will go directly to protecting the local marine environment. **Cayo de Agua**, to the south of the archipelago, is considered to have one of the world's most beautiful beaches. However, not all the Los Roques Islands are open to tourists—many, in fact, are completely off-limits to visitors to keep them pristine.

Above: One of the many large shells you'll find washed up on the shores in Los Roques. Right: Little gulls live a charmed and completely protected life on the deserted islands in the Los Roques chain.

CUA DAI

QUANG NAM

Hoi An Beach, which lies about 2.5 miles east of the historic town, is a southern extension of the famous China Beach at Da Nang, which became famous in 1992 after the first surfing competition was held there and which was a favorite R&R destination for American soldiers during the Vietnam War.

Cua Dai Beach is on the South China Sea and is an attraction for both locals and tourists. The Victoria Hoi An Resort has to be the most luxurious and charming place to stay in the entire area. A fun atmosphere and a relaxed ethnic mix have made this beach very popular—it's very lively at night thanks to its little bars and superb seafood restaurants. There are always street vendors around selling kites, drinks, and local sweets, and romantic couples strolling the sand. Until just a few years ago, one of the big attractions on the beach was Darling, a female elephant that lived at the Victoria Resort and was universally adored by children who enjoyed rides on her that invariably ended up with a dip in the sea. Poor Darling is no longer with us and Cua Dai hasn't found any replacement for her. However, every evening, on the area in front of the Victoria Resort, oil lamps are lit and big comfortable triangular cushions are laid out on rush mats along the silky white beach so that guests can watch the hundreds of little boats out lamping octopuses and shrimp. At the southernmost tip of Cua Dai is the estuary of the river Thu Bon. At sunset, and with tide permitting, you'll see the Hoi An fishing boats in a spectacular line that has a ritual-like quality to it. Where the sea and river waters join, in fact, you'll see another truly unique type of traditional fishing method involving very fine nets that are cast to the wind like sails by the fishermen. A few miles away are the Cham Islands, little granite rocks topped with tropical rain forest. Their turquoise bays are nicely protected from the monsoons and are home to a few little fishing villages—they make a very interesting boat trip for tourists enjoying Cua Dai.

NEARBY

Don't miss the morning market along the jetties and wharfs of the **Thu Bon River**, which surrounds and defends the old town center of **Hoi An**. Take a trip by Vietnamese junk at dawn or sunset along the banks of the river and down through the estuary and into the open sea. The old town of Hoi An is a UNESCO World Heritage Site and has wonderful old warehouses, Chinese temples, and workshops where artisans spend their days making charming paper lanterns. Around 30 miles from Hoi An is the spectacular **My Son**, a Cham dynasty capital between the 4th and 12th centuries AD. It was home to more than 78 **Cham towers** and temples before the Vietnam War. You can't leave without going to the **fish market** at Hoi An—it attracts hundreds of fishermen and buyers.

Opposite: Traditional kites sold on the always lively beach at Cua Dai. Left: An elephant ride on the famous Darling, who lived at the Victoria Resort in Hoi An for many years.

Beaches are the perfect place to tap into the life force unleashed by the oceans. Everyone has their own way of doing it. Some, like the surfers on Bondi or Waimea Beach, have an almost symbiotic relationship with the waves. They're happy to wait for hours for the "big one" that will push them to the very edge of physical limits. Others prefer to hike for miles along vast stretches of sand laid bare by the retreating tides. The French beaches—Grand Plage in Biarritz and Le Touquet—are ideal for that. Sometimes it's the wind that provides the energy, filling sails and sending them scudding across the waves, adding that extra something to a game of volleyball or tennis or a climb on the Calanques in the Mediterranean and Pacific.

Dario Bragaglia

SPORTS
beaches

BONDI BEACH
NEW SOUTH WALES

I t looks like a scene out of the legendary 1978 surfing movie *Big Wednesday*. But there's no Gary Busey anywhere to be seen. Dozens of smiling, beautifully toned young men and women proudly stroll down to the water with their surfboards under their arms. Others cluster together in small groups, locked in animated debate. They're deciding when and where to go into the water and what strategy they use to ride the 20-foot waves. Bondi is the most famous beach in Australia, host nation to the 2000 Olympics. Young women and families with children sunbathe and watch the surfing spectacle unfold. The lifeguards scan the beach with their binoculars from the top of the lookout towers, making sure that everything is running smoothly. Their gaze lingers over the sea as they admire the surfers riding the walls of water and then gliding straight into the tunnels. In the distance, they can hear the noise of Sydney, the financial, commercial, and cultural capital of Australia as well as the continent's oldest city. Campbell Parade runs along the beach and throbs with people. This is a happy, lively, often barefoot community with a cosmopolitan feel to it. There are restaurants of all kinds, bars serving surfer seafood and surfer breakfasts of yogurt and exotic fruit, specialist shops where surfers buy and rent boards and wetsuits. At the Bondi Surf Company you can even check the weather forecast in real time and find out what the sea conditions are like and how big the waves will be. The name Bondi in the ancient language of the Aborigines means "where the sea breaks over the rocks." In our 21st-century world, the beach has an almost mystical concentration of surfers. The twirling boards, the crashing of the sea, the sense of freedom, and the build-up to the waves give a real sense that, here at least, man is truly at one with the power of nature.

NEARBY

Sydney is just a 20-minute drive away and, with Melbourne, is one of Australia's largest cities. There's plenty to see and do: take a trip to the 1,580-acre **Olympic Park** built for the 2000 Games and now used for major sports and cultural events. Then there's the **aquarium**, home to over 2,000 different species and an incredible array of sharks; the 1,152-foot-high **Sydney Tower**, whose top two stories rotate; the legendary Jorn Utzon **Opera House**, a landmark in 20th-century architecture and officially opened by Queen Elizabeth in 1973 (it has an organ with 10,500 pipes and was declared a World Heritage Site in 2007).

Above: The Sydney Opera House, declared a UNESCO World Heritage Site in 2007. **Right:** *Bondi Beach attracts huge crowds of Sydney's younger generation as well as surfers from all over Australia.*

JERICOACOARA
CEARÀ

Even though there are few truly unexplored areas of the globe left, there remain certain remote spots that can still surprise and excite even the most jaded of travelers. So if you feel the need to have your faith in our planet renewed, take a trip to the northeast of Brazil and have a look around between Parnaiba and Camocim, in the states of Piauí and Cearà. Base yourself in the fishing town of Camocim, where life is still simple, the boats sport multicolored sails, and the salty smell of freshly caught fish drifts in the air. The Boa Vista Resort was built by entrepreneurs from Verona in Italy and is a great place from which to explore the charming little coastal villages such as Jericoacoara and its dune-lined beach. You can get there by off-roader—the last few miles will take you along the shore. This is something of a glittering gem in a sea of white sand, coconut palms, magnificent rock formations, and clear, freshwater lakes.

A timeless fishing village rechristened Jeri by the first adventurous hippies to discover it more than 30 years ago, Jericoacoara is still exceptionally charming and is considered one of the world's most beautiful beaches. The local sailboats, *jangadas*, still work out of here alongside the modern-day windsurfing boards. While villages now have electricity and the fishermen's cabins have been converted into cute *pousadas*, this is very much a place where everyone wanders around barefoot on the sandy roads. Only off-roaders can cope with the latter so the pace of life is gentle. Apart from its endless beach and surfer-perfect wind, Jeri has a host of stores selling beautiful artisan wares made by the local ladies, who still weave by hand. Sunset is caipirinha time—this delicious drink is made with *cachaça* (a local liquor distilled from sugar cane) and will keep you having fun until dawn. Don't miss the spectacle of the *dunas acesas* or the famous *pedra furada*, a natural sea arch. Your last port of call of the night will be to *la Padaria* for hot cheesy bread and coffee. Everyone knows everyone in Jeri and you'll soon feel right at home there.

NEARBY

You can't leave without enjoying the thrill of riding the endless dunes in a dune buggy. This area is known as the Brazilian Sahara but unlike the African Sahara, has rivers, lakes, and the sea. The landscape is ever-changing and unexpected, the shore incredibly long, and pigs, cattle, and donkeys roam freely inland. Slide down the dunes and straight into the water at **Praia de Maceió** and **Lago do Boqueirão**. Or enjoy the excitement of a tumble in one of the rough little wooden sleds. Drink in the pristine beauty of the **Praia do Xavier**, a picturesque fishing village, visit the superb ecosystem that is the **Barra dos Remédios**, and also **Lago Verde** at **Tatajuba**, one of the most beautiful beaches in northeastern Brazil.

Above: A group of young Brazilians doing the capoeira, *a ritual dance that mimics warrior-like movements.* **Opposite:** *The sand dunes at Jericoacoara are dozens of yards high and run all the way down to the sea.*

PLAYA TAMARINDO
NICOYA

NEARBY

The **Peninsula de Osa** is one of the most inaccessible and fascinating parts of Costa Rica. It is located on the Pacific coast and includes the **Parque Nacional del Corcovado**, which itself is home to the only surviving stretch of rain forest in the western Pacific area. The park covers a massive 106,210 acres and has hundreds of species of trees, jaguars, snakes, and insects living within its borders. Just near the entrance to the Parque del Corcovado, you'll see the **Isla di Cano**. Its exotic underwater rock formations have helped create a truly magnificent ecosystem teeming with hundreds of different species of fish and crustaceans, including a native lobster and a huge mollusk, the giant conch.

Steven Spielberg chose Costa Rica to shoot the opening scenes of *Jurassic Park* and it's not hard to see why he made the effort to come here. The country's lush, primordial landscape of endless forests and plains seem to float over a cobalt sea with rivers winding their lazy way through grasslands crisscrossed by orange dirt tracks. The area has a stunning biodiversity thanks to government protection for the last 30 years and 75 reserves making up 27 percent of the entire country.

This small state is one of the few nations in the world that really does live in harmony with nature and is a favorite destination with eco-tourists because of its pristine and primordial landscape. In its 31,000 square miles, it has numerous protected habitats that span the entire spectrum from mountain chains to savannah, rain forests to mangrove swamps, islands, deserted beaches, and coral cliffs. Tiny villages peep out from between the banana and coffee plantations. Gentle canals run through the jungle, mountains seem to embrace the landscape itself as waterfalls tumble and roar. The beaches are white—and black. But apart from all that, Costa Rica also has one of the most famous surfing beaches in the world, which attracts legions of fans from all over the globe.

Familiar from a host of TV ads and movies, Playa Tamarindo is in the northwest, just above Santa Cruz. It's such a ready-made surfing paradise that many American and European surfers have actually moved here so that they can spend every day out on the water. Playa Tamarindo really does, quite literally, offer life on the crest of the wave. Playa Tamarindo has fabulous hotels and great bars to relax in after a hard day in the water. You can try a number of other sports there as well: sailing, kayaking, wet biking, boogie boarding, horseback riding, and big game fishing. Speaking of the latter, the fishing for record-breaking marlin, tuna, and dentex is superb. Nearby is the Playa Grande, where the lute turtles, which can weigh up to 660 pounds and are the world's largest, come to lay their eggs.

Above: Playa Tamarindo is a beach made in heaven for surfers and a favorite with Americans and Europeans alike. **Opposite:** *The shape of the bay and the gently sloping shore mean that the waves are ideal for surfing and boogie boarding.*

CABARETE
PUERTO PLATA

There's room for everyone at Cabarete, a small fishing village in the north of the Dominican Republic, about 22 miles from Puerto Plata. Every day the sky becomes a stage, the beach an audience, and the sea a curtain. Hundreds of kiteboarders gather to provide a spectacle that sweeps visitors off their feet. The weather conditions are perfect: the hot trade winds that come from the east can reach 25 knots; light currents that carry you towards the shore; the absence of dangerous fish; and a splendid bay marked out by a coral reef. Every year the Kiteboarding World Tour comes here. An international cast of devotees gathers to perform acrobatics in the sea. It's also possible to practice windsurfing or diving. Even novices can experience the emotion of riding the waves: there are many instructors here who give both private and group lessons, especially in the morning, when there's less wind and the sea is calm. Those who prefer to take it easy, on the other hand, can sunbathe on the fine white sandy beach. In the evening the Playa Cabarete becomes a veritable dance floor, coming to life to the rhythm of salsa and merengue. Restaurants, bars, and cafés place tables and couches outside and offer fish-based meals, as well as the more famous Dominican cocktails: mojito, cuba libre, and daiquiri. Between cocktails there's also time for shopping in the assorted arts and crafts shops, many of which are right on the beach. Here you can find the *munecas sin rostro*, the faceless dolls that are almost a symbol of the Dominican Republic and of the union of its three main ethnic groups: indigenous, African, and European.

NEARBY

Not far from the center of Cabarete, you will find the **El Choco** national park, a botanical garden featuring medicinal plants and fruit teas. Here you can go trekking or horseback riding. Yet the main attraction comes in the form of the **three grottoes**, which were discovered 30 years ago. In the first, which is small and dark, there are stalagmites and stalagtites. In the second, which is larger, the portrait of a Taino god is clearly visible. Here the inhabitants of the surrounding area take cover during the hurricanes. The third, on the other hand, is 80 feet deep and is connected to a natural water swimming pool, where swimmers can dive without difficulty.

*Above: Full kite surf sails off the beach of Cabarete. **Right**: Windsurfing is popular in the waters of Cabarete, thanks to the coral reef which protects the bay from the wind.*

EGYPT

MANGROVE BEACH
RED SEA

NEARBY

South of the protected area of Wadi El Gemal is the ancient city of **Berenice**, founded by Ptolemy II in 275 BC. It is flanked by 60 miles of unspoilt coastline with palms, mangroves, and 37 miles of wadis, which spread out into the desert. One very interesting excursion is the historic emerald and gold mines which date back to the 5th and 6th centuries. Mining was first begun by the pharaohs to the southwest of Marsa Alam. You'll get a real feel of Africa in **Shalateen**, a timeless spot on the Sudan border (220 miles from Marsa Alam) where one of the largest camel markets in Upper Egypt is held. It's also a gathering place for the Basharee, Ababda, and Rashida tribes.

This white and pink beach dazzles the eyes and enchants the soul. Made of millions of seashells ground to dust by the waves, it is rimmed by a deep blue reef and mangroves reaching off into the distance. Mangrove Beach is dotted too by white sandy dunes and incredibly pristine nature. Its waters are breathtakingly clean and colorful, and then on the mountainous side of it are canyons, wadisk, a lunar landscape, and amber rock. Located on the road between Marsa Alam and the Sudan border, it is perfect for snorkeling, swimming in the lagoon, and sipping tea in one of the nearby Bedouin tents. The Marsa Alam coast may be heaven indeed for snorkeling, diving, and kite surfing enthusiasts but it's an equally wonderful place to take a relaxing morning stroll. The beach itself is around 100 yards from the barrier reef, which runs parallel to the shore, and the water depth ranges from 1 to 13 feet. The reef also runs parallel to the shore. In some stretches, you can get to the reef from the shore but in others there are jetties. Diving here is a truly unique experience: fantastic views, coral-covered peaks, sea fans, madrepore, starfish, and shoals of tropical fish that burst with color and life. You'll see parrot fish and butterfly fish swimming in pairs, clown fish hiding in the anemones, and bat fish slithering into rocky cracks. Down on the sea floor, ray, gray mantas, napoleon fish, and moray abound. The water temperature is sublime. This area has it all: archaeology dating back to the pharaohs, the underwater world of the Red Sea, gorgeous landscape, eco-tourism, desert excursions, and exotic treatments in the resort spas using ionized sand, oils, and therapeutic sulfur.

The best diving is around the El Kula'An Islands, a string of coral atolls that make up little white sandy islands. For example, there is Ado Dabab Bay, home to the dugong (cow of the sea), a protected marine mammal that looks like an enormous seal. You'll also see dolphins, turtles, and ospreys. There are delightful marine and inland excursions from Safaga, Qusier, and Port Ghalib as well.

Above: A stretch of beach in Mangrove Bay complete with sun loungers and sun umbrellas. **Opposite:** *A dugong, a protected marine mammal, and a sea turtle.*

Founded by the Greeks in 600 BC, Marseille is a city of the sea, fine architecture, art, culture, good food, great wine, and much more, especially sports. France's largest port is surrounded by wonderfully varied and stunningly beautiful countryside.

The Calanques jut out into the sea like long fingers, their 15 miles of jagged white limestone rock contrasting starkly with the deep blue of the sea and the green of the local maquis. These Mediterranean fjords are similar to those between Calvi and Porto on the island of Corsica, and are home to dozens of gorgeous inlets: l'Oule, Morgiou, Sugiton, Les Goudes (289 climbing routes), Callelongue, Sormiou (a wide sand and shale beach with compact rocky sides), Deverson (the highest cliffs), Port Pin, and Port Miou (the deepest). However, the wildest and most atmospheric of all, with its tiny, lonely little expanse of white sand, is definitely En Vau. Les Calanques are France's 10th national park and are a paradise for pleasure sailors as they offer excellent shelter and anchorage. They are over 13,000 years old and are topped by some of France's finest trekking trails. You'll find rare species of both flora and fauna and see peregrine falcons gliding through the air, as this is the natural habitat of both the latter and the eagle owl. The best place to use as a base for exploring this wonderful area is the town of Cassis, 12 miles to the east of Marseille (the Calanques actually separate them). This small fishing port of 8,000 souls has everything: trekking trails, diving, free climbing 960-foot-high calanques that drop straight into the sea. There's also canyoning, potholing, rafting, and all kinds of other excursions to choose from. Sports and big sporting events are a feature of Marseille life and that of the surrounding area—they've hosted everything from the Tour de France à la Voile to the Louis Vuitton sailing regattas, tennis tournaments, beach volleyball, beach rugby, and beach soccer.

NEARBY

For a truly dizzying experience, take a drive down to **Cap Canaille,** where you'll find **Cap Dirty,** one of Europe's highest cliffs. It lies to the east, between Cassis and Ciotat, and affords absolutely breathtaking views of the bays, promontories, and islands. The **Cosquer Cave** is a geological treasure in its own right and is decorated with art and carvings dating back dozens of millennia when the sea level in this area was 350 feet lower. Unfortunately it's now closed to visitors for safety reasons. You can't leave **Marseille** without a visit to the cathedrals, forts, and arsenals that provide a daily reminder of the city's fiery past. Don't miss the docks, which were given a new lease on life by architect Eric Castaldi, and **Boulevard Longchamp.**

*Left: The wonderfully deserted beach at En Vau nestled between the steep canyon-like walls of the Marseille Calanques. **Opposite:** Free climbing is one of the big attractions on this stretch of coastline.*

GRAND PLAGE
BIARRITZ (AQUITAINE)

Biarritz: the surfing capital of Europe or fashionable French Second Empire summer resort? Two very different worlds collide in the modern tourist version of this delightful town on France's Atlantic coast. From its early days as a tiny whaling village, Biarritz officially morphed into the 19th century's chicest summer resort after Victor Hugo declared in 1843: "I don't know any place as enchanting as this!" In reality, however, the town's transformation was actually due more to Eugénie de Montijo, consort of Napoleon III, who summered there. The empress also gave Biarritz a magnificent palace, now the Hotel du Palais, and the nearby Byzantine cupola of the Chapelle Imperiale. This paved the way for the town to become the most fashionable royal destination of the day. Queen Victoria herself vacationed here in 1889, after which it became one of the favorite retreats of Edward VII, King of Great Britain and Ireland. Other leading European monarchs, such as Alfonso XIII of Spain and Sissi of Austria, were frequent visitors, too. Biarritz was also an attraction for intellectuals and writers of the day, including Dumas, Stendhal, Zola, and Flaubert. Intriguingly, at the end of the 1950s, Biarritz discovered a previously unimagined vocation for surfing, which brought it a new lease on life. Introduced from California in 1957 by the author and screenwriter Peter Viertel, surfing proved a major hit on the Continent and Biarritz soon earned a reputation as "Europe's surfing capital." The town now hosts a string of international competitions that attract the world's top surfers. It also has no less than 30 surf schools—more than there are in California, in fact. More laidback visitors can choose to simply stroll along the Grand Plage, a wonderful expanse of powdery pink sand overlooked by the casino, and watch the dozens of surfers carving up the waves.

NEARBY

Explore the local hills, villages, and delicious Basque cuisine on foot, by automobile, or on one of the small indigenous Pottock ponies. Local dishes to sample include: *chipirons* (squid cooked in its own ink), *piperade* (scrambled eggs with tomatoes and peppers), *zikiro* (lamb broiled on a wood fire), and the famous *pintokos* (Basque *tapas*). The Atlantic coast offers a choice of excursions, too: **Saint Jean de Luz**, the former whaling port where Louis XIV married Infanta Maria Teresa of Spain; **San Sebastian**, renowned for its film festival; the **Guggenheim Museum** in Bilbao; the 233-foot Biarritz **Light,** which dominates **Cap Hainsart**.

Above: The Grand Plage stretches out in front of Biarritz Casino. ***Right:*** *Surfers intent on riding the long ocean waves that break on Biarritz beach.*

LE TOUQUET
NORD-PAS-DE-CALAIS

Almost 6 miles of sandy beach running along the Côte d'Opale, France's northernmost shore-line. On clear days, you can even see the blurry outline of England in the distance. London is actually nearer than Paris and there is a certain Anglo-French ambivalence to the culture and architecture of the resort town of Le Touquet. In 1874 Hippolyte de Villemessant, founder of the *Le Figaro* newspaper, had the idea of transforming a stretch of sand dunes into a vacation resort for the Paris beau monde, calling his creation Paris-Plage (Paris on the Beach). However, it was actually two Englishmen, John Whitley and Allen Stoneham, who turned the luxury resort into a sports para-dise when they put Pierre de Coubertin, father of the modern Olympics, in charge of it. Between the late 1800s and early 1900s Le Touquet was given what were fabulous facilities for the day, including a horse racing track, golf, and tennis courts. However, the most popular sport in Le Touquet today is actually *char à voile* or sail karting, which enthusiasts enjoy on the huge expanses of beach exposed at low tide. Even with only a couple of hours of instruction, you can have a huge amount of fun in these breathtaking contraptions (wear a helmet and prepare yourself for inevitable spills as well as thrills). Needless to say, the wind is excellent for sailing at sea. Le Touquet Paris-Plage also enjoys a reputation as a year-round resort. Each February, in fact, thousands of motorbikes come here to compete in the Enduro des Sables watched by 280,000 spectators. In April, the town hosts the Côte d'Opale mara-thon and the Pro Am at the golf club. There are also many other tennis tournaments, horse racing events, and car rallies held against the town's backdrop of beach and forest, making Le Touquet one of France's prime sporting destinations.

NEARBY

Boulogne is the town from which Napoleon intended to depart to invade England in the early 1800s. It lies just a few miles north of Le Touquet and is nowadays split into the lower town, one of Europe's largest fishing ports, and the Haute Ville, still ringed by the 13th-century walls erected on the ruins of the original Gallo-Roman ones. The town inside the walls is lovely as well: the castle now houses an Egyptian museum, the basilica of Notre Dame, and il Beffroi dell'Hotel de Ville. Don't miss a visit to **Nausicaa,** a center dedicated to the sea, which will be a hit for anyone traveling with children.

*Above: The long expanse of sand at Le Touquet plays hosts to sports of all kinds. **Right**: Sail karting is one of the most popular—and exciting—activities on Le Touquet beach.*

CLIFTON BEACH
WESTERN CAPE

NEARBY

Don't miss the suburbs of **Sea Point, Camps Bay,** and **Llandudno,** not to mention the little fishing village of **Hout Bay**. This is a good starting point for reaching the nature reserve of **The Cape of Good Hope**. This was where the Dutch pioneers dropped anchor on their way to **Cape Point**, South Africa's south-westernmost point. If you take the funicular railway you can reach the lighthouse in order to admire the marvelous scenery below. But for a complete view of Cape Town, you need to go to the top of **Table Mountain**. This is a unique experience, as this is a protected area with a high concentration of flora and fauna.

Imprisoned like underwater canaries, in order to meet the white shark face to face. At Clifton Beach, the most fashionable in Cape Town, a breathtaking encounter with one of the sea's most ferocious killers is all part of the fun. You just need to climb into a steel cage in order to come into contact with these terrifying predators.

The more courageous athletes come here to try their hand at cage diving. This experience is within everyone's reach: you take a boat a few miles offshore, you put on a frog suit and oxygen tank, and you plunge into the crystal clear water. Sooner or later the white sharks will appear. Their curiosity is aroused by the intruders, and some of them will even stick their noses into the cage. The more foolhardy divers can't resist the temptation to stroke them above their awesome jaws. For those of you who are less keen on taking risks, this splendid South African beach also lends itself to lengthy kayak excursions: these will enable you to discover hidden inlets or, better still, to admire Table Mountain, Cape Town's greatest attraction. And the ocean's great waves prove irresistible for lovers of windsurf and kite surf. Sailboats can take advantage of the constant wind, while this is also a favorite hang-out for scuba divers. And it's pretty difficult to get bored on the beaches here. There are four of them. They are all sandy, divided by granite rocks, and protected from the wind. They don't actually have precise names: Fourth, which is for families with small children, is a blue flag beach; Third and Second are popular with youngsters; First is the wildest and has the fewest visitors. To reach them you simply follow the coast road, Victoria Road, and climb down the steps to the beach. This is a wonderful place for young people who take each other on at rugby, soccer, beach volleyball, Frisbee, and racketball, under the burning sun.

*Above: The broad gulf of Clifton Beach, which consists of four beaches and is a favorite spot for South African youth. **Opposite:** Clifton Beach has something for everyone, from the peace and quiet of Fourth Beach to the sporting intensity of Second.*

South Beach, known locally as SoBe, is Florida's most famous strip of shoreline and the pride of the city of Miami. Its pale, silky sandy shore stretches for 3 long miles and is lapped by the Atlantic Ocean. The beach itself is framed by the gorgeous backdrop of Ocean Drive's Art Deco architecture, giving it a unique appeal. SoBe's regulars include both residents and sports-loving vacationers. Physical activity is part of the way of life here and the elegant beachfront hotels are favorites of fashionistas and celebrities. Needless to say, South Beach has a long movie resumé spanning everything from *Miami Vice* (naturally) to *Scarface*. The area is also home to many actors and over 1,500 models. Beach volleyball and Frisbee are favorite games out on the sand, but in quieter corners you'll see people doing yoga. The **Ocean Drive** sidewalks are busy with joggers, roller-bladers, skateboarders, and cyclists. One of SoBe's biggest attractions is its subtropical climate, which means you can swim here in the depths of winter. It's the perfect destination for watersports lovers. You won't get the same waves as in the Pacific but neither sailors nor surfers will go away disappointed either. There's also waterskiing and you can rent out clear-bottomed kayaks, canoes, banana boats, jet skis, and even big game fishing boats. If you go snorkeling or diving you'll see parrot fish, nurse shark, green moray eels, and lots of lobster. There's a natural coral reef to explore and various wrecks which provide perfect habitats for a wide variety of marine life. Artificial barrier reefs were also created starting in the 1980s with the same idea. Don't miss exploring the delightful South Beach Underwater Park. And if the sea alone isn't enough for you, there's also a big sky over South Beach that's perfect for parasailing and kite surfing. The main thing, however, is to follow the SoBe philosophy of keeping fit and looking good, and why not? There are plenty of spas in the area as well.

NEARBY

Take in a Miami Dolphins football game at the **Dolphin Stadium** in Greater Miami. Check out the Marlins, the local baseball team. A trip to the track is always fun and there's plenty of that at **Hialeha Park Race Track**, which has a delightfully retro look to it. There are endless courses for golfers, including the **Doral** and the **Biltmore Hotel**. It's also worth following the coast north from South Beach along Collins Avenue and the A1A to Hollywood, where there's a boardwalk with bike and jogging paths. **Lauderdale by the Sea** also has a lovely palm-edged beach, white sand, and not a skyscraper in sight (they're banned) as well as the 1950s-style **Anglin's Pier**. The whole of **Greater Fort Lauderdale** offers superb diving, too.

*Above: Surfing is one of the most popular sports in Florida in general and at South Beach in particular. **Opposite:** The action never stops on Ocean Drive, which runs along the beach and throbs with neon all night long.*

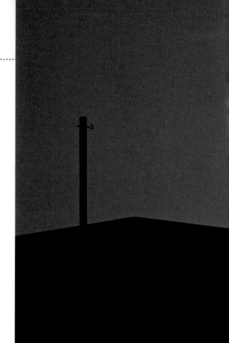

USA

VENICE BEACH
CALIFORNIA

The name alone is the stuff of legend: Venice Beach. It's a busy, beautiful stretch of shore in a district of Los Angeles designed by Abbot Kinney in the early 20th century along the lines of the original Renaissance-era city, complete with canals, gondolas, and arching bridges. Even today, Venice Beach is a main attraction for tourists drawn here by the town's reputation as a refuge for Hollywood stars who flee here to escape Beverly Hills, and enjoy Venice's Baywatch towers, picture postcard-perfect sunsets, and vicinity to Santa Monica and Malibu. Then, of course, there's the popular boardwalk with its Frank O. Gehry architecture. However, once you get there, either by Venice Road or the faster Santa Monica Freeway, you'll find yourself swept up on the beach itself in an instant. The Ocean Front Walk is a wonderfully eclectic meeting point and showcase. At more or less set times each day, defenders of good causes, mostly pacifists and members of the Salvation Army, give vent to their opinions in open competition with the more commercial ventures going on around them. Once you've managed to work your way past the human barricade, you'll realize it's a busy spot teeming with beach volleyballers, joggers, cyclists, and crowds of other people using the simple but very efficient facilities of this enormous and highly democratic outdoor gym. Venice is a busy place where celebrities mingle with joggers, while gorgeous girls in-line skate past bodybuilders, aging hippies, and business people fleeing the Los Angeles trade shows. This extravagant town was given a new lease on life by the Los Angeles administration in the 1980s. Enormous murals abound in this wonderful melting pot. Venice is a natural-born stage and a place where everyone and anyone will feel at home and at peace with themselves.

NEARBY

This is the home of kitsch and so there's no escaping a trip to the **Muscle Beach**, an open-air gym owned by the legendary Hulk Hogan. Then, prepare yourself to be blown away by Canadian Frank O. Gehry's binoculars, a stunning building that now houses the Chiat-Day-Mojo advertising agency (340 Main Street). There's a wonderful mix of tourists and local residents along the bike paths and streets. Don't miss the **Jim Morrison mural** on 17th Place and the former site of the POPO or **Pacific Ocean Park**, a futuristic theme park that once rivaled Disneyland in popularity.

*Above: A serpentine network of bike and pedestrian paths runs behind Venice Beach. **Right**: One of the famous Baywatch towers on Venice Beach, a place where anything goes.*

The plane has hardly come to a standstill at the end of the Reef Runway and the pilot hasn't even started taxiing towards the terminal building, but you can already hear the sound of Hawaiian music on board. "Honolulu baby, where d'you get those eyes... I want to go back to my little grass shack at Kealakekua... beyond the reef." Hawaii welcomes and seduces tourists from all over the world with its musical harmonies and sea breezes. The air in the islands is filled with the intense aroma of plumeria (or frangipani) so poignant it will make you dizzy with delight. "Aloha!" says a red, white, and blue sign, which points towards customs: "Welcome to Hawaii, USA." "Aloha!" is everywhere, from the escalators to the airport exit, where the *wahine* (Hawaiian women), with their long, tawny hair and dark eyes, place garlands of orchids around the necks of tourists.

The island of Oahu is the largest in the Hawaiian archipelago, which is situated in the middle of the Pacific Ocean. It is considered the world's most remote land mass. Here East meets West in a kaleidoscope of colors, nature, hula girls, discos, soap

NEARBY

On the island of Oahu you will find **Waikiki**, arguably the world's most famous beach. It's possible to see all the island's principal attractions in one day. You can visit the **Bishop Museum** with its collection of Hawaiian art; **Diamond Head**, the island's most famous natural attraction; **Kawaiaha'o Church**, consecrated in 1882 and built entirely of coral; the **National Memorial Cemetery of the Pacific**, the final resting place of the victims and veterans of World War II, the Korean and Vietnam Wars. And last, but not least, **Pearl Harbor**, scene of the famous Japanese attack on the US Navy. Kewalo Basin is the starting point for visits to the **USS Arizona Memorial**.

Above: The colors of a sunny day at Waimea Bay. **Left**: A group of surfers wait for the right wave to come along. **Opposite**: The shape of the gulf and the sandy seabed ensure that the waves are long and regular and therefore perfect for surfing.

opera memories, creation legends, Shinto temples, and surfing clubs. That's right, because surfing was born here, in Waimea Bay. It's a story that has been well documented down through the years. No lesser an authority than Captain James Cook, the man who discovered Hawaii, tells us in his diary of 1778: "As I observed the native penetrate the long waves near Waimea Bay on a board... I could not help concluding this man had the most supreme pleasure while he was being driven so fast and so smoothly by the sea."

It is clear that surfing or the surfboard was considered a test of human strength and intelligence against the power of nature. In actual fact the surf or wave board (in Hawaiian, *he'e nulu*, literally "sliding on the waves") represents man's ability to dominate the ocean. The technique consists of gliding on a board which appears to be glued to the surfer's legs, along the wall of the wave, which can reach heights of more than 32 feet in some cases, before crashing against the beach. Expert surfers are capable of carrying out a series of acrobatic moves whose complexity will depend on the height and the arch of the waves. If Captain Cook was enraptured by this particular sporting discipline, then the same cannot be said of the Calvinist missionaries, who reached the archipelago in the wake of the great explorer. Horrified by the nudity of the natives as they rode the waves, they banned surfing on the grounds that it was immoral. The sport enjoyed something of a revival in the late 19th and early 20th century, however, much of the credit for which

must go to Duke Kahanamoku, a swimming champion who gave demonstrations of his surfing abilities on the American and Australian coasts. The surfing technique has evolved since the mid-1980s, particularly in terms of speed and aerial maneuvers, thanks to the invention of the short board. This is narrower and more tapered and it has three fins on its keel, as opposed to one. At Waimea Bay, thanks to its fantastic tubular waves, it's easy to see spectacular surfing moves: tube riding, for example, which consists of facing the wave while being covered by its upper lip, before gliding out of a tunnel of water the moment before it crashes closed.

Opposite: Tropical vegetation surrounds the beach at Waimea Bay. *Above*: Hawaii is synonymous with surfing. *Right*: A storm at Waimea Bay.

Their remote locations, rarified beauty, and almost mystical solitude make this group of beaches very special. They're the kind of places that bring out the wanderlust in us all. Scattered around the world, they all have different flora and fauna and cultural backgrounds. But their names are the stuff of dreams: Palmetto Point, Barbuda; Tayrona National Park, Colombia; Qalansya, Yemen; Balos, Crete; Beriknica, Croatia; Girolata, Corsica; Punta Pirulil, Patagonia. Each one of these gorgeous beaches shares a unique allure and visual impact. These are the icons of nature at its most pristine and remind us of how privileged we are to be there, in their intense beauty and purity. Long may they remain.

Beatrice Spagnoli

UNREACHABLE
beaches

PALMETTO POINT
SAINT KITTS AND NEVIS

Palmetto Point is a long ribbon of sand running along the ocean's edge where the magical coral island of Barbuda, lively Antigua's more laidback cousin, stands silent guard over sailors heading out to open sea. It's also home to one of the world's most beautiful and remote beaches. Antigua has no less than 365 natural beaches—one for every day of the year. There are also numerous coral reefs along its southern and eastern shores, and these shelter the bays to the extent that you can always swim regardless of the wind. Barbuda is a small island of 100 square miles of sand and palms. More importantly, it is a genuine oasis of peace and tranquility. Its western coast is lined with fabulously sandy beaches including Gravenor Bay, much loved by snorkeling enthusiasts who flock there for the variety of coral formations nestling in its depths. The most famous of all Barbuda's beaches runs from Palmetto Point as far as Cedar Tree Point. It's only reachable by sea, and in the first light of dawn it turns a delicate pink because of the tiny seashells washed ashore by the tide. Few experiences can beat the thrill and beauty of sailing into Palmetto Point after a long 12-hour overnight passage from Antigua. It lies at the very end of a gentle bluff that itself is the southernmost point on the island, not far from Codrington Lagoon. Palmetto Point is a place for genuine sea and nature lovers as more or less the only thing to do is take long walks along the shore, which just goes on forever—look out for conch shells at sunset. Alternatively you could just stretch out in the sun and allow the steady cool breeze to caress your skin or enjoy lengthy swims in the calm turquoise waters of the coral reef that shelters the beach from the waves.

NEARBY

Barbuda's many other beaches include the enchanting sandy expanse of **Gravenor Bay**, beloved by snorkelers who come for the coral formations. It's a huge bay which runs east-west between Coco Point and Spanish Point. There's also a big lagoon north of the Bay. The only sounds that will disturb your idyll here will be from the birds, which include breathtaking frigates ("eagles of the sea"). Barbuda actually has the largest colony of these magnificent creatures in the entire Caribbean. Gravenor Bay turns pink at dawn each day because of the countless tiny seashells washed up there by the tides.

Above: Palmetto Point is a beach on Barbuda and can only be reached by sea. *Right:* The spectacular Palmetto Point, with its pristine expanse of sand stretching off into the distance.

PUNTA PIRULIL
CHILOÉ

"Our ocean, the planet's largest and roughest with waves 20 feet higher than any other, seems to have made the crescent of sand at Cucuo its playground. In the inlets and cracks, the rhythm of three small resting waves and three big working ones changes, creating an unexpected wave, the seventh waves much-awaited and feared by the men out hunting for seals or gathering shellfish." The words of Francisco Coloane, Chiloé's most famous son, give us an incisive glimpse of what the deserted western coast of this stormy island holds in store.

Your trek to Punta Pirulil begins south of Cucao at the gateway to the Parque Nacional. It's a secret place you're heading for. A lonely, legendary, gold-panners' paradise. You'll trek for half a day to get there along an endless dark shale and sand beach scattered with shells and *cochayuyo*, an edible seaweed that's collected at low tide. At Rahue-La Montaña the hills stretch right down to the shore. Streams crisscross them, lagoons glitter, gigantic gunnera plants flourish. There's a thick green carpet of chacay and brush beaten flat by the merciless wind. The clouds race across the sky letting the occasional ray of sun light shine through as the Pacific spray clothes the promontories and sea stacks in a salty fog. You get the feeling that Moby Dick is about to come roaring out of its depths at any moment. There's always the chance that you might come across the seductive Pincoya, a beautiful and generous water nymph reputed to wander the shore bestowing prodigious gifts on the *Chilote*.

The writer Bruce Chatwin was awestruck by the wild stories told by the Chilote elders, which he called a "stew of tormented mythologies": the Boatman of the Souls in the village of Huillinco, the basilisk, mermaids, the King of the Earth who stole all the animals from Cucao. "What am I doing here?" this restless wanderer asks himself in his final notebook. Never was there a better question.

NEARBY

Awarded UNESCO World Heritage status, the **150 wooden churches** on the island of Chiloé are simple and modest. Built from the mid-1800s onwards by the Jesuits and later the Franciscans, they are genuine works of art and play a dual role. Firstly they are of course places of refuge for the faithful during the religious ceremonies held on the island, and secondly their bell-towers provide a reference point for sailors and seafarers. Their dark, dusky interiors provide magnificent testament to the skills of the local carpenters. The warmth of their wood feels cozy and inviting as the wind howls outside. Don't forget to check out the capital, **Castro**, with its multicolored wooden houses on stilts.

Opposite: The long, deserted beach at Punta Pirulil. Left: A stretch of the beach at Punta Pirulil, which is streaked by waves and water, and edged by lush marine vegetation.

ARRECIFES

MAGDALENA (TAYRONA PARK)

Thus far, Tayrona National Park in Colombia has managed to avoid the hand of man. It's a unique nature reserve at the foot of the Sierra Nevada de Santa Marta, near the world's highest sea. And it really is paradise, with 7,400 acres of beach rimming the coral barrier reef and alternating with rain forest, mangrove swamps, and palm groves. You will find yourself trekking through what seems like endless dense jungle, which will suddenly open up on a tropical beach of soft white sand and towering palm trees with colorful hammocks strung between them. A huge contrast to the blue of what is a genuinely crystal clear sea. The path enters the reassuring density of a palm grove and then pops out again at the sea, this time edged by big rounded Atlantic rocks. Then, a mountain appears in the distance but you'll have to scale its 2,500 feet to get to a settlement of a local tribe descended from the Tairona, the nation's largest group of indigenous people. It is in these mountains that the Tairona's culture flourished and they became renowned goldsmiths. Theirs is the Ciudad Perdida (Lost City), which was rediscovered in the 1970s. Only a few descendents of these ancient people now survive, and most work in the park. Visitors can also, having gained the required permits, stay in their traditional stone and wood huts (the roofs are made from palm leaves). The most famous inlets are Concha, Chengue, Gayraca, Neguange, Cinto, Guachaquita, Palmarito, and Cañaveral. Baia Concha and Cañaveral are the most popular and have restaurants, services, and campsites. There are watersports and diving at Baia Concha. You can swim in the inlets but caution is advised as there are strong currents, particularly at Cañaveral. The fact that its landscapes are so varied and a constant year-round temperature (82–86°F) make Tayrona National Park the perfect natural habitat for over 100 species of rare birds and mammals, including condors and eagles.

NEARBY

About 21 miles from Tayrona National Park, you'll come to the **Sierra Nevada de Santa Marta** range, which includes Colombia's two highest peaks, **Picos Colón** and **Bolívar**. These mountains have unique biodiversity and are home to the Kogi, Arhuaco, and Arsario people. They slope right down to the Atlantic Ocean creating magnificent inlets. Founded by Rodrigo de Bastidas in 1525, Santa Marta is Colombia's oldest city. It was also the home of the Libertador Simon Bolivar and is thus of some historical interest. Archaeology lovers can follow paths traced by the indigenous Tairona people before the arrival of the Spanish conquistadors and explore the fascinating sites at **Chengue, Neguange, El Cedro**, and Nosevé.

Opposite: Huge rounded rocks and silky sandy beach at Arrecifes. **Left**: A brightly colored toucan, an inhabitant of the Tayrona National Park.

BALOS
CRETE

The Venetian castle on the islet of Imeri Gramvousa dominates the Balos lagoon in north-western Crete from a height of 438 feet. Some believe that this is the island of the god Aeolus and that Odysseus stopped here and received from him a gift of winds to release as he made his way back to Ithaca. The triangular castle harks back to days when the island needed defending against invasions by the Turks and pirates. Both the castle and the island itself are now very much returned to nature and provide a protected habitat for unique species of both flora and fauna. Migratory and hunting birds, monk seals, turtles, wild donkeys, and 26 endemic species of plants now live here (a total of 400 species of plants has been catalogued). To get to the dazzlingly white Balos beach, you'll have to tackle a very tricky and slightly hair-raising cliff-top path. Drive from Kissamos-Kastelli to Kaliviani, where you'll take a dirt road in the direction of Cape Vouxa as far as the Church of Agia Irini. You'll have to walk from there on a path that wanders through thyme, juniper, mastic, and carob beaten flat by the strong winds. You'll finally get to the top of 500 steps leading down to the beach. Be warned, however: walking back up in the sun is exhausting. The lagoon's waters are tinged pink by shell fragments. They're warm and shallow in the enclosed areas. However, if you look inward you'll see a Mediterranean-type landscape that turns rocky and barren. In fact, the 2,438-foot Mount Geroskinos can be snow-capped right into April. The lagoon and the island can also be reached by sea from Kissamos-Kastelli—stick close to the Gramvousa Peninsula and you'll see how the western end of the island of Crete has risen from 19 to 29 feet above its level in ancient times while the eastern end nearer to Turkey has subsided.

NEARBY

After spending the day enjoying the sea at Balos, you'll have worked up an appetite for dinner in one of the traditional *tavernas* in this historic area of Crete. Just a 10-minute drive south of Kissamos-Kastelli, you come upon the ancient town of **Polyrinia**, perched on the top of a 1,340-foot hill. Dating back to Minoan times, Polyrinia was one of ancient Crete's most heavily fortified towns and dominated the entire western part of the island. Ruins of much of the old town walls remain and you'll literally have a glimpse of history as you nibble on your Greek salad at one of the tables outside the **Taverna Acropolis**.

Above: The characteristic lunar landscape of the Balos lagoon. **Right:** *The island of Gramvousa with the Venetian castle, which can be seen from Balos beach.*

BERIKNICA
ISLAND OF PAG

No sooner have you crossed Paski Most, the land bridge linking the mainland to the island, that a majestic scene unfolds before you. A dazzling rock plunges into a deep blue sea: the contrast is surreal, breathtaking. You are on the steep and inaccessible side of the island of Pag, which runs along the coastline for a good 37 miles. This long corridor is known as Bad Weather Channel because of the *bora* wind which reigns supreme here in winter, sometimes hitting peaks of 80 mph and beyond. It also sweeps down on the rest of the island covering it with salty spray. "Even the locals get pungent," confesses a fisherman from Metajna, rather vaguely.

Wherever the *bora* hits, the landscape is barren, bitter, and desert-like. Sage and thistle are the only plants that somehow manage to survive the onslaught. The beach is farther ahead, on the eastern coast of Paski Zaliv, a stretch of inland sea that opens into the Adriatic through Pag Island's own strait, Paska Vrata. Remote and cut-off, Beriknica is really best reached by boat—you can charter one from the island's main town, also called

NEARBY

Located about a half mile from **Metajna**, the nearest town, this bay is the start and end point for the hiking trail to Beriknica beach. You can drive there, and it has to be said that the Grill Canyon bar and restaurant makes it a bit cozier than the rather secluded Beriknica. The restaurant specializes in fish caught by the owners themselves or brought in by the local fishermen. A carpet of pebbles slopes gently into the turquoise water. Its temperature in August gets up to a warm 77°F, making it perfect for families with small children. The bell rung by the "bar-boat," which regularly washes up on the beach, will wake you just as you doze off.

*Above: The crystalline colors of the waters at Pag Island. **Left:** The stunning beach at Rucica, which has a very unusual geometric shape. **Opposite:** A corner of the enchanting beach at Beriknica.*

Pag or Metajna. Alternatively, you can drive around Paski Zaliv at Rucica beach where the road peters out. Leave your car there and trek through the lunar landscape for an hour or so. This scenic area is known as Stone Canyon and affords stunning views. Rock formations stripped bare by the wind and whitened by spray line the route.

The barren white-gold karst rock is flayed by the northwesterly wind and plunges into a crystalline sea that is a beautiful deep blue in its deeper spots. The lunar landscape is somewhat relieved by flocks of sheep wandering here and there, their fleeces blending in with the color of the rock itself in a unique form of camouflage. It's the kind of rather lonely place, however, that it's a relief to see other living creatures in.

Hidden by a large inlet, this is a wide, clean pebble beach. If you look around you, you'll feel you're right at the center of an enormous, intensely colored pumice stone that seems to be suspended just over the sea.

Majestic and disturbing griffon vultures whirl soundlessly in the sky above while, on the eastern side, tiny free climbers cling to the superb peak that juts up above the rest of the landscape. Because it is so difficult to get to, the beach tends to be really quite empty even in August—with just a few tourists and fishermen around. The visitors that come by boat tend to be best equipped with food, drink, and sun umbrellas while hikers usually have to travel a lot lighter. If you take a stroll around you'll get a closer look at the odd rock formations—they're made up entirely of fossil agglomerate, including the large masses near the shore and the characteristic peak. The shadow of the rocky spur at the western end of the bay starts to lengthen from early afternoon onwards and after a few hours covers the entire area, causing visitors to pack up and leave. If you don't want to have to negotiate Stone Canyon for the second time in the same day, you can easily hitch a lift back to your car at Rucica with one of the boats pulled up on the beach. This bus-boat experience is unusual but a fun way to get around. Once you arrive back at the car park, you'll find yourself looking at the path you took earlier in the day with a twinge of regret. It may have been tough but it was worth every spectacular, memorable minute!

Opposite: A fisherman and his traditional fishing boat in an inlet on the island of Pag. **Above:** Another view of the beach at Beriknica. **Right:** The pebble beach at Beriknica.

GIROLATA

CORSICA

Girolata is a breathtaking beach but not one for the faint-hearted. There are no roads leading there so you'll have to go by boat out of Porto, or on foot. If you choose the hike it'll take you two hours along a mule track flanked by Mediterranean maquis from Col de la Croix. Whatever you do, don't forget to bring some water—all that walking is thirsty work—and you might also play with the idea of stopping off at Tuara beach for a cooling dip. However, as you round the last bend in the track, the Gulf of Girolata will open up before you in all its beauty. A small bluff topped by a Genoese tower, a sort of fairy-tale castle perched on a cliff-top with a few houses around it, a eucalyptus grove, and crystal clear sea washing up against a pebble beach. This is the wildest part of Corsica's coastline and an absolute dream for geologists: great slabs and hunks of basalt, porphyry, and rhyolite jut out of the sea like huge marine milestones. The result of ancient volcanic eruptions, they've been sculpted by wind and sea into peculiar shapes. The waters teem with a huge variety of fish that dart right up to a few yards from the shore. Overhead, sea eagles, cormorants, and other marine birds glide across the clear blue sky. When you arrive at the isolated little other-worldly village of Girolata, the only sounds you'll hear are the hum of the wind and the rhythmic beat of the waves. The poignant perfume of the Mediterranean brush floats up in the air and you'll gaze down on views that make you feel like you've been transported back to medieval times. This utterly wild remote part of the world was once a favorite haunt of pirates and in fact it was here that the infamous corsair Dragut was captured by the Genoese fleet commanded by Giannettino Doria, grandson of the legendary Andrea Doria.

Between June and September the atmosphere in Girolata livens up greatly but between dusk and dawn the little village returns to its true magical, silent self. A genuine natural paradise.

NEARBY

While Girolata offers a small foretaste of heaven, you'll get a much larger one if you push on just a few more miles to the **Scandola Nature Reserve**, 5,000 acres of protected coastline and waters, home to threatened flora and fauna, such as the sea eagle. Together with Girolata, the nearby Gulf of Porto, and Les Calanques de Piana, this park was awarded World Heritage Site status in 1982. Even diving and close-up photography of its wildlife are prohibited. You just can't get to Scandola on foot and it's not always easy by sea, either. However, if the conditions are right, you should make the effort, as taking a boat trip around the reserve is an unforgettable experience.

Above: The Genoese tower overlooking the promontory of Girolata. **Opposite:** *The small beach at Girolata nestled among its characteristic reddish rocks.*

Pantelleria juts out of the Mediterranean Sea just 52 miles from Cap Bon in Tunisia. This wild volcanic little isle is a dark beauty and rimmed by a jagged, treacherous coastline. Its rocks, caves, sea arches, and cliffs are largely accessible only by sea. There are very few places that can actually be reached overland and even then it's a struggle. The only safe harbor for boats when the sirocco pick up is the Cala Cinque Denti or Bay of the Five Teeth. You'll have to negotiate a steep and rather uneven footpath running through the rocks, but when you do get there, you're in for a very pleasant surprise: a cobalt blue sea enclosed by a wall of jagged rocks. You can easily swim around the little sea arch after which you'll find yourself in a natural pool called the Scarpetta di Cenerentola (Cinderella's Slipper). Here the water is as clear as an aquarium, revealing orange and purple rocky walls with glints of silver. If you walk back up the coast road, you won't have to stray too far from Cala Cinque Denti before you come upon the spectacular lava dome known as Khaggiàr.

Brilliant green foliage flourishes between the broken lava rocks, which are as black as coal. The effect at sunset is stunning. Weird rocky formations emerge from the carpets of succulent plants and look like witches, prehistoric animals, and rabbits frozen in eternal contemplation of the sea. It is also well worthwhile taking a walk down the dirt road in the direction of Punta Spadillo.

You'll be surrounded by huge lava formations hewn by the wind and the poignant scent of wild fennel, myrtle, and rosemary as you arrive at the Laghetto dei Gamberi (Shrimp Pond), a kind of a natural swimming pool of sorts where you'll be able to take a dip even when the sea is rough. Farther on you'll find the Laghetto delle Ondine (Lake of the Ondines), another rock pool filled by the northerly tides. This is a great place to just stretch out and soak up the sun.

NEARBY

If you'd like to discover the beauty of the island's interior, you'll have to take the *Perimetrale* or coast road that runs right around its edge. It's only 25-miles long but it takes in everything from ancient *dammusi* to well kept vineyards. Beyond the **Sesi Archaeological Park** at Mursia, you'll come to the **Sataria** thermal baths, where legend has it that Ulysses made love to the nymph Calypso. Hike up to the **Montagna Grande,** which overlooks the Valle di Monastero, and just lose yourself in the pines, wild oregano, and myrtle. Don't forget to pay a visit to the *favare* (fumaroles). Take the road towards Bugeber and enjoy gazing down on the emerald sulfurous waters of the **Specchio di Venere** (Venus's Mirror).

Above: Fishermen aboard a colorful traditional gozzo fishing boat off Pantelleria.
Opposite: The jagged coastline and deep blue sea of the Cala Cinque Denti.

LOVE AND DIVORCE BEACH

BAJA CALIFORNIA

NEARBY

You can drive back along the Transpeninsular highway from Los Cabos through cactus-dotted desert as far as Loreto. From there you can take a boat out to the **Isla Coronado** to swim with the sea lions, the island's only inhabitants along with some dolphins. This is one of the prettiest of all the islands in the Sea of Cortez. On two sides the island has high rocky cliffs but on the other two there are white sandy little coves. Delightfully, between the balmy months of January and March, Baja California plays host to gray whales migrating from the Bering Strait to give birth in warmer climes. Don't miss a visit to **Bahia de Los Angeles,** where there are dolphins and whale sharks.

Baja California is a 1.5-mile-long Mexican peninsula. The landscape there is wild, primitive, and desert-like. Huge expanses of earth and sand stretch out in the distance. The only plants anywhere to be seen are cactuses. Just on the edge of the horizon is the gleam of the sea: on one side lies the Pacific Ocean and on the other, the Sea of Cortez. It is crossed by the Transpeninsular, a highway that winds its way through a spectacular backdrop of coves and canyons. A trip through the canyon leading to Los Cabos on the very tip of the Baja is an almost spiritual experience. Very calming. By the time you finally get to Cabos San Lucas, your soul will be filled with the peacefulness of your surroundings. It's hot here but the steady sea breeze means it's always just pleasantly so. You won't find a souvenir, fruit, or sombrero seller here that won't suggest a visit to the legendary Los Cabos Arch, the area's main attraction, which is renowned world wide as the Love Beach. Or more accurately, according to the locals, Love and Divorce Beach. It's hard to grasp where this spot gets that name until you actually get here. Something we might add, you can only get there by sea, but have no fear there is a local taxi boat service. The boats come to within a few yards of the shore, unload their passengers in the water, and then turn around and head off. At this point, you'll realize why this place is called the Beach of Love: the fine silky sand is a delicious apricot color and rimmed by rocks that look like twisted gargoyles. Spreading out before you is the turquoise Sea of Cortez, whose wonderful colors seem to melt into the sky itself. Seagulls whirl overhead and silence reigns supreme. At the right end of the beach is a natural red stone arch. Beyond it, the waves turn rough. That's because this is the Pacific Ocean with its huge, wind-swollen waves. Not a place for a swim. But to the locals, this wind- and wave-swept beach represents the other side of matrimony—the side that ends in divorce. Hence the beach's double nickname. Legend has it that if an engaged couple visits both sides, they'll have a happy marriage because they'll realize they have to avoid the treacherous bickering that would ruin their relationship.

Above: A gray whale in the waters of the Baja California. ***Opposite:*** *Love Beach with the Sea of Cortez on one side and the Pacific Ocean on the other.*

QALANSYA
SOCOTRA

The off-roaders can't get down as far as the sea, so they unload their passengers at the bottom of a small dirt hill road that seems purpose-built to stimulate a hiker's curiosity. Up top, a truly breathtaking scenario unfolds. Tall rock juts out around a beach that snakes doodle-like into the turquoise water. Qalansya beach is made from sand as silky soft as talcum powder. It is just immense and hemmed in by a crown of beautiful but very solid rocky ochre hills that flame an almost surreal red at sunset. In summer, when the monsoons batter this bit of coast on Socotra, a Yemeni island floating between the Gulf of Aden and the Horn of Africa, the sand drifts up against the rocky walls bit by bit until dunes begin to form. These are compact little pyramids, genuinely architectural shapes that give the landscape an unique look. Seen from afar they resemble virgin snow whose pristine beauty no one dares besmirch. Towards evening, the crabs come out of hiding and make their way in droves towards the water on Qalansya beach, leaving behind the incredible spiral lairs they've carved out for themselves that leave the beach dotted with neatly arranged and identical heaps of sand.

NEARBY

Declared a UNESCO Biosphere Reserve, **Socotra** is home to the comical-looking little bottle tree, and to the Dragon's Blood tree, the latter being very much the symbol of the island. Socotra's beauty lies in its wild heart and unique vegetation (there are no less than 300 native flowers), which has never been contaminated in anyway, nor have its plants interbred with any non-native species. This has a lot to do with the total **biological isolation** that the island enjoyed for 6 million years—it was, in fact, inaccessible until a very short time ago. Initially a British protectorate, then a Soviet marine base until 1967, it could not be reached because there were no connecting flights until 2002.

*Above: A typical bottle tree. **Left**: A school of local dolphins who live in the waters around the island. **Opposite**: A spectacular shot of the beach at Qalansya, the pride and joy of the island of Socotra.*

The sea birds all flock in then and perch on this little crescent of sand jutting out into the sea. Seashells are something the island of Socotra has a lot of. You'll rarely see so many shells in one place anywhere else in the world. There are so many different kinds, shapes, and sizes, all strewn out there on the sand. Please do resist the huge temptation to just scoop some up and take them home. They are part of what makes this island special, like its incredibly hospitable inhabitants. These are people quite unused to tourism as we know it: and luckily so, as a place this pristine and unspoilt deserves to stay that way.

You'll often see what looks like a river of silver gleaming in the sea just a little out from shore: a school of dolphins leaping and diving and twisting through air and sea with effortless grace.

The sea around Socotra is rich in marine life with 800 different species of coral and 730 types of tropical fish. Needless to say, it's something of a mecca for divers but it's equally pleasurable for ordinary swimmers, too. As soon as you step into the water, you'll be surrounded by shoals of tiny fish so colorful they look hand-painted. You'll often find yourself being approached by a local fisherman who'll offer you wonderful chunks of warm fish he's just caught and cooked. He probably lives in a cave on the coast, somewhere near the edge of the beach. You will also find other local people selling shells that they have patiently cleaned and polished themselves.

Qalansya would be a fantastic beach for the entire family—it's huge and very safe.

Unfortunately, it's also very out of the way. The only way to cross the island is by off-roader, often down very narrow, rough trails. You'll have to camp out on the beach or in the *funduk*, a sort of boarding house with simple rooms and rather slapdash hygiene. But Socotra's magic lies in its primitive nature, its purity. Its pristine pyramid-like dunes run on along the west coast from Qalansya, and are probably best appreciated by taking a boat trip to the magnificent and incredibly private beach at Ahrar. The vegetation is unusual, too. All elements that combine to make this island truly unique.

Opposite: *A colony of birds foraging for food on the sandy shore.* **Above**: *The rocks on Socotra blaze a fiery red at sunset.* **Right**: *The natural rock sculptures on the beach.*

TRAVEL
information

BRIGHTON

Name	Brighton
Country	United Kingdom
Region	East Sussex
Nearest town	Brighton and Hove
Language spoken	English
Local currency	Sterling
Average temperatures	41–50°F winter, 59-71°F summer
Vaccinations required	None
Type	Pebble
Dimensions	Length 7 miles, width up to 50 yards
Facilities	Equipped areas and all kinds of services along Esplanade
Suitable for families/kids	Yes
When to go	June to September

CALA SAONA

Name	Cala Saona
Country	Spain
Region	Formentera
Nearest town	None
Language spoken	Spanish
Local currency	Euro
Average temperatures	50–57°F winter, 80–86°F summer
Vaccinations required	None
Type	Sand
Dimensions	Length half mile, width 300 yards
Facilities	Sun umbrellas, sun loungers, bar, hotel
Suitable for families/kids	Yes
When to go	June to September

CANNON BEACH

Name	Cannon Beach
Country	United States
Region	Oregon
Nearest town	Portland
Language spoken	English
Local currency	US dollars
Average temperatures	39–50°F winter, 71–79°F summer
Vaccinations required	None
Type	Sand, coral reef, palm trees
Dimensions	Length 7 miles, width up to 200 yards
Facilities	Catering and tourist facilities
Suitable for families/kids	Yes
When to go	July to September

CHE CHALE

Name	Che Chale
Country	Kenya
Region	Malindi
Nearest town	Malindi
Language spoken	Swahili and English
Local currency	Kenyan shilling
Average temperatures	82–86°F
Vaccinations required	None
Type	Fine white sand
Dimensions	Length 17 miles, width up to 40 yards
Facilities	Only at resorts
Suitable for families/kids	No
When to go	July to March

CHOWPATTY

Name	Chowpatty
Country	India
Region	Maharashtra
Nearest town	Mumbai
Language spoken	Hindi, English, Marathi, Gujarati
Local currency	Indian rupee
Average temperatures	60–95°F
Vaccinations required	None
Type	Sand
Dimensions	Length half mile, width up to 200 yards
Facilities	No
Suitable for families/kids	No
When to go	September to April

COPACABANA

Name	Copacabana
Country	Brazil
Region	Rio de Janeiro
Nearest town	Rio de Janeiro
Language spoken	Portuguese
Local currency	Brazilian real
Average temperatures	77–86°F
Vaccinations required	None
Type	Sand
Dimensions	Length 2.5 miles, width up to 60 yards
Facilities	Sun loungers, sun umbrellas in some areas, and refreshment services
Suitable for families/kids	Yes
When to go	November to March

GENIPABÙ

Name	Genipabù
Country	Brazil
Region	Rio Grande do Norte
Nearest town	Fortaleza
Language spoken	Portuguese
Local currency	Brazilian real
Average temperatures	71–80°F
Vaccinations required	None
Type	Sand and large dunes
Dimensions	Length around 6 miles, width varies
Facilities	Tourist and sports facilities
Suitable for families/kids	Yes
When to go	November to March

HAT SAI KAEW

Name	Hat Sai Kaew
Country	Thailand
Region	Koh Samet
Nearest town	Rayong
Language spoken	Thai, English
Local currency	Baht
Average temperatures	86–89°F from January to April, 68–82°F from November to December
Vaccinations required	None
Type	Fine white sand
Dimensions	Length half mile, width up to 50 yards
Facilities	Sun umbrellas, refreshments
Suitable for families/kids	Yes
When to go	Year-round

HAYARKON BEACH

Name	Hayarkon Beach
Country	Israel
Region	Tel Aviv
Nearest town	Tel Aviv
Language spoken	Hebrew
Local currency	Shekel
Average temperatures	50–57°F winter, 71–80°F summer
Vaccinations required	None
Type	Fine sand
Dimensions	Length 600 yards, width up to 50 yards
Facilities	Sun loungers, sun umbrellas, refreshments, private beach areas
Suitable for families/kids	Yes
When to go	June to September

JIMBARAN BAY

Name	Jimbaran Bay
Country	Indonesia
Region	Bali
Nearest town	Kuta
Language spoken	Bahasa Indonesia and English
Local currency	Rupee
Average temperatures	68–86°F
Vaccinations required	None
Type	Sand
Dimensions	Length around 2.5 miles, width up to 50 yards
Facilities	Only at resorts
Suitable for families/kids	Yes
When to go	April to September

JUMEIRAH BEACH

Name	Jumeirah Beach
Country	United Arab Emirates
Region	Dubai
Nearest town	Dubai
Language spoken	Arabic and English
Local currency	EAU Dirham
Average temperatures	64–68°F winter, 82–91°F summer
Vaccinations required	None
Type	Sand
Dimensions	Length 2 miles, width up to 100 yards
Facilities	Deckchairs, sun loungers, leisure and sports facilities, refreshments
Suitable for families/kids	Yes
When to go	November to April

PLAYA DE LA BARCELONETA

Name	Playa de la Barceloneta
Country	Spain
Region	Catalonia
Nearest town	Barcelona
Language spoken	Catalan
Local currency	Euro
Average temperatures	41–57°F winter, 64–80°F summer
Vaccinations required	None
Type	Sand
Dimensions	Length half mile, width up to 90 yards
Facilities	Beach center, showers, volleyball, skating, ping pong, playground
Suitable for families/kids	Yes
When to go	June to September

TYLÖSAND

Name	Tylösand
Country	Sweden
Region	Halland
Nearest town	Halmstad
Language spoken	Swedish
Local currency	Swedish crown
Average temperatures	32–48°F winter, 68–75°F summer
Vaccinations required	None
Type	Sand
Dimensions	Length 4 miles, width up to 200 yards
Facilities	Deckchairs, sun umbrellas, bar, private beach areas, showers, life guard
Suitable for families/kids	Yes
When to go	June to September

BAHÍA GARDNER

Name	Bahía Gardner
Country	Ecuador – Española Island
Region	Galápagos Islands
Nearest town	None
Language spoken	Spanish
Local currency	US dollar
Average temperatures	71–77°F
Vaccinations required	None
Type	Sand
Dimensions	Length 1 mile, width up to 200 yards
Facilities	No
Suitable for families/kids	Yes
When to go	October to May

MARINA DI RAVENNA

Name	Marina di Ravenna
Country	Italy
Region	Emilia-Romagna
Nearest town	Ravenna
Language spoken	Italian
Local currency	Euro
Average temperatures	41–46°F winter, 77–82°F summer
Vaccinations required	None
Type	Fine sand
Dimensions	Length 2 miles, width 250 yards
Facilities	Private beach areas, 250 playing fields (beach volleyball, tennis)
Suitable for families/kids	Yes
When to go	May to September

SEVEN MILE BEACH

Name	Seven Mile Beach
Country	Jamaica
Region	Westmoreland
Nearest town	Negril
Language spoken	English
Local currency	Jamaican dollar
Average temperatures	77–86°F
Vaccinations required	None
Type	White sand
Dimensions	Length 7 miles, width up to 100 yards
Facilities	Sun loungers, Sun umbrellas, resort, dive centers, refreshments
Suitable for families/kids	Yes
When to go	December to April

ACCIAROLI

Name	Acciaroli
Country	Italy
Region	Campania
Nearest town	Salerno
Language spoken	Italian
Local currency	Euro
Average temperatures	39–53°F winter, 62–82°F summer
Vaccinations required	None
Type	White sand
Dimensions	Length 1 mile, width up to 40 yards
Facilities	Sun loungers, sun umbrellas, games for kids, bar
Suitable for families/kids	Yes
When to go	April to October

MORRO DE AREIA

Name	Morro de Areia
Country	Cape Verde
Region	Boa Vista
Nearest town	Sal Rei
Language spoken	Portuguese and Creole
Local currency	Cape Verde escudo
Average temperatures	77–79°F
Vaccinations required	None
Type	Sand
Dimensions	Length around 2 miles, width 400 yards
Facilities	No
Suitable for families/kids	Yes
When to go	Year-round

SUPER PARADISE

Name	Super Paradise
Country	Greece
Region	Mykonos
Nearest town	None
Language spoken	Greek
Local currency	Euro
Average temperatures	52–59°F winter, 84–91°F summer
Vaccinations required	None
Type	Sand and pebble
Dimensions	Length 300 yards, width 50 yards
Facilities	Sun loungers, sun umbrellas, private beach areas, bar
Suitable for families/kids	No
When to go	June to September

ANSE LATIO

Name	Anse Latio
Country	Rep. of the Seychelles
Region	Praslin
Nearest town	None
Language spoken	Creole, French, and English
Local currency	Seychelles rupee
Average temperatures	82–86°F
Vaccinations required	None
Type	Fine sand
Dimensions	Length 1 mile, width up to 200 yards
Facilities	None
Suitable for families/kids	Yes
When to go	March to May

CALA MITJIANA

Name	Cala Mitjiana
Country	Spain
Region	Balearic Islands
Nearest town	Mahòn
Language spoken	Spanish and Menorquin
Local currency	Euro
Average temperatures	60°F winter, 77°F summer
Vaccinations required	None
Type	Fine sand and cliffs
Dimensions	Length 100 yards, width 50 yards
Facilities	No
Suitable for families/kids	No
When to go	May to September

CAP DE LA HAGUE

Name	Cap de la Hague
Country	France
Region	Normandy
Nearest town	Cherbourg
Language spoken	French
Local currency	Euro
Average temperatures	42–50°F winter, 62–68°F summer
Vaccinations required	None
Type	Sand and cliffs
Dimensions	Length 5 miles, width up to 200 yards
Facilities	Campsite, sailing school
Suitable for families/kids	No
When to go	March to September

GOLDEN BEACH

Name	Golden Beach
Country	Northern Cyprus
Region	Famagosta
Nearest town	Famagosta
Language spoken	Turkish and Greek
Local currency	New Turkish lira
Average temperatures	61–68°F winter, 82–91°F summer,
Vaccinations required	None
Type	Sand and dunes
Dimensions	Length 3 miles, width up to 400 yards
Facilities	Refreshments only
Suitable for families/kids	Yes
When to go	March to October

IS ARUTAS

Name	Is Arutas
Country	Italy
Region	Sardinia
Nearest town	Cabras
Language spoken	Italian
Local currency	Euro
Average temperatures	68–75°F May to September
Vaccinations required	None
Type	Quartz grains and cliffs
Dimensions	Length half mile, width up to 50 yards
Facilities	Campsite, car park, bar
Suitable for families/kids	Yes
When to go	May to September, not August (too crowded)

CALETA VALDÉS

Name	Caleta Valdés
Country	Argentina
Region	Chubut
Nearest town	Puerto Madryn
Language spoken	Spanish
Local currency	Argentinean peso
Average temperatures	39–50°F winter, 68–77°F summer
Vaccinations required	No
Type	Gravel
Dimensions	Length 15 miles, width up to 70 yards
Facilities	No
Suitable for families/kids	Yes
When to go	June to September

CAPE RANGE

Name	Cape Range
Country	Australia
Region	Western Australia
Nearest town	Exmouth
Language spoken	English
Local currency	Australian dollar
Average temperatures	59–68°F June to October, 64–80°F November to May
Vaccinations required	None
Type	Sand and cliffs in areas
Dimensions	40 miles of coast
Facilities	Only in ecolodge areas
Suitable for families/kids	Yes
When to go	November to May

GOUKAMMA

Name	Goukamma
Country	South Africa
Region	Western Cape
Nearest town	Knysna
Language spoken	English
Local currency	Rand
Average temperatures	41–57°F April to October, 71–77°F November to March
Vaccinations required	None
Type	Sand and cliffs
Dimensions	Length 3 miles, width up to 100 yards
Facilities	Campsite, hostel, refreshments
Suitable for families/kids	Yes
When to go	November to March

LA DOUBLE

Name	La Double
Country	Corsica
Region	Cavallo Island
Nearest town	None
Language spoken	French
Local currency	Euro
Average temperatures	44–53°F winter, 73–82°F summer
Vaccinations required	None
Type	Sand
Dimensions	Length 30 yards, width 10 yards
Facilities	No
Suitable for families/kids	Yes
When to go	May to September

IERANTO

Name	Ieranto
Country	Italy
Region	Campania
Nearest town	Massa Lubrense
Language spoken	Italian
Local currency	Euro
Average temperatures	39–53°F winter, 62–82°F summer
Vaccinations required	None
Type	Sand, pebble, and limestone cliffs
Dimensions	Length 20 yards, width 10 yards
Facilities	None
Suitable for families/kids	No
When to go	Year-round

PLAYA BLANCA

Name	Playa Blanca
Country	Mexico
Region	Yucatan
Nearest town	Cancún
Language spoken	Spanish
Local currency	Mexican peso
Average temperatures	62–77°F from May to October, 80–86°F November to April
Vaccinations required	None
Type	Sand, very fine coral
Dimensions	Length 6 miles, width 1 mile
Facilities	Only at hotels
Suitable for families/kids	Yes
When to go	May to September

PRAIA DO FORTE

Name	Praia do Forte
Country	Brazil
Region	Bahia
Nearby	Salvador
Language spoken	Brazilian, Portuguese and English
Local currency	Brazilian real
Average temperatures	77–86°F
Vaccinations required	None
Type	Fine sand and rocks
Dimensions	Length 7 miles, width 12 Yards
Facilities	A few sun beds and paid sun loungers
Suitable for families/kids	Yes
When to go	Year-round

TORRE SALSA

Name	Torre Salsa
Country	Italy
Region	Sicily
Nearest town	Agrigento
Language spoken	Italian
Local currency	Euro
Average temperatures	50–59°F winter, 86-95°F summer
Vaccinations required	None
Type	Fine white sand, dunes
Dimensions	Length 3 miles, width up to 150 yards
Facilities	Visitors' center and windsurfing
Suitable for families/kids	Yes
When to go	March to October

BURTON BRADSTOCK

Name	Burton Bradstock
Country	United Kingdom
Region	England
Nearest town	Lyme Regis
Language spoken	English
Local currency	Sterling
Average temperatures	37–46°F winter, 65–70°F summer
Vaccinations required	None
Type	Sand
Dimensions	Length 3 miles, width up to 100 yards
Facilities	No
Suitable for families/kids	Yes
When to go	May to September

RABIDA

Name	Rabida
Country	Ecuador
Region	Galápagos
Nearest town	Puerto Baquerizo Moreno
Language spoken	Spanish
Local currency	US dollar
Average temperatures	62–90°F
Vaccinations required	No
Type	Red sand
Dimensions	Length 50 yards, width 20 yards
Facilities	No
Suitable for families/kids	Yes
When to go	June to December

ANAKENA BEACH

Name	Anakena Beach
Country	Chile
Region	Rapa Nui
Nearest town	Anakena
Language spoken	Spanish and Rapa Nui
Local currency	Chilean peso
Average temperatures	68–75°F
Vaccinations required	None
Type	Sand, white coral
Dimensions	Length 200 yards, width up to 50 yards
Facilities	Kiosks from March to December only
Suitable for families/kids	Yes
When to go	March to December

CALA D'ARENA

Name	Cala d'Arena
Country	Italy
Region	Sardinia
Nearest town	Sassari
Language spoken	Italian
Local currency	Euro
Average temperatures	46–59°F winter, 68–80°F summer
Vaccinations required	None
Type	White sand
Dimensions	Length 30 yards, width 10 yards
Facilities	No
Suitable for families/kids	No
When to go	May to October

SHROUD CAY

Name	Shroud Cay
Country	Bahamas
Region	Exuma
Nearest town	George Town
Language spoken	English
Local currency	Bahamian dollar
Average temperatures	77–86°F
Vaccinations required	None
Type	Fine white sand
Dimensions	Length around 1 mile, width varies
Facilities	Hotels, dive centers, big game fishing
Suitable for families/kids	Yes
When to go	Year-round

BELLES RIVES

Name	Belles Rives
Country	France
Region	Provence
Nearest town	Antibes-Juan les Pins
Language spoken	French
Local currency	Euro
Average temperatures	41–55°F winter, 73–80°F summer
Vaccinations required	None
Type	Hotel beach – boardwalk
Dimensions	Length 100 yards
Facilities	Sun umbrellas, bar, restaurant, waterskiing
Suitable for families/kids	Yes
When to go	April to September

CASTELFUSANO

Name	Castelfusano
Country	Italy
Region	Lazio
Nearest town	Rome
Language spoken	Italian
Local currency	Euro
Average temperatures	68–82°F
Vaccinations required	None
Type	Sand
Dimensions	Length 3 miles, width 50 yards
Facilities	Some stretches of private beach areas, sun loungers, car parks and bar
Suitable for families/kids	Yes
When to go	May to October

DAYANG BUNTING

Name	Dayang Bunting
Country	Malaysia
Region	Langkawi
Nearest town	Kuah Town
Language spoken	Malay and English
Local currency	Ringgit
Average temperatures	68–90°F
Vaccinations required	None
Type	Fine sand, tropical vegetation
Dimensions	Length 400 yards, width around 30 yards
Facilities	Refreshments and public restrooms
Suitable for families/kids	Yes
When to go	October to May

ELIE

Name	Elie
Country	United Kingdom
Region	Scotland
Nearest town	Elie
Language spoken	English
Local currency	Sterling
Average temperatures	37–39°F winter, 64–71°F summer
Vaccinations required	None
Type	Sand
Dimensions	Length 1 mile, width up to 300 yards at low tide
Facilities	Sailing and windsurfing center
Suitable for families/kids	Yes
When to go	June to August

IPANEMA

Name	Ipanema
Country	Brazil
Region	Rio de Janeiro
Nearest town	Rio de Janeiro
Language spoken	Portuguese
Local currency	Brazilian real
Average temperatures	77–86°F
Vaccinations required	None
Type	White sand
Dimensions	Length 2 miles, width up to 200 yards
Facilities	Kiosks, private beach areas, showers, sun loungers, sun umbrellas
Suitable for families/kids	No
When to go	November to March

MARINA BEACH

Name	Marina Beach
Country	India
Region	Tamil Nadu
Nearest town	Chennai (Madras)
Language spoken	Tamil, English, and Hindi
Local currency	Indian rupee
Average temperatures	75–95°F
Vaccinations required	No
Type	Sand
Dimensions	Length 6 miles, width up to 200 yards
Facilities	No
Suitable for families/kids	Yes
When to go	November to February

OM BEACH

Name	Om Beach
Country	India
Region	Karnataka
Nearest town	Gokarna
Language spoken	Hindi
Local currency	Rupee
Average temperatures	77–90°F
Vaccinations required	None
Type	Sand and cliffs
Dimensions	Length half mile, width around 20 yards
Facilities	None
Suitable for families/kids	No
When to go	Year-round

PAMPELONNE

Name	Pampelonne
Country	France
Region	Provence
Nearest town	Ramatuelle
Language spoken	French
Local currency	Euro
Average temperatures	46–54°F winter, 77–82°F summer
Vaccinations required	None
Type	Sand
Dimensions	Length 3 miles, width up to 50 yards
Facilities	Sun loungers, sun umbrellas, bar
Suitable for families/kids	Yes
When to go	May to September

PROMENADE DES PLANCHES

Name	Promenade des Planches
Country	France
Region	Normandy
Nearest town	Deauville
Language spoken	French
Local currency	Euro
Average temperatures	39–46°F winter, 60–68°F summer
Vaccinations required	None
Type	Fine sand and boardwalk
Dimensions	Length 1 mile, width 500 yards
Facilities	Sun umbrellas, private beach areas, refreshments and watersports center
Suitable for families/kids	Yes
When to go	June to September

PURI

Name	Puri
Country	India
Region	Orissa
Nearest town	Puri
Language spoken	Hindi and English
Local currency	Rupee
Average temperatures	61–95°F
Vaccinations required	Anti-typhoid recommended
Type	Fine white sand
Dimensions	Length around 6 miles, width up to 150 yards
Facilities	Only kiosks and stalls
Suitable for families/kids	No
When to go	October to March

RAMLA BAY

Name	Ramla Bay
Country	Malta
Region	Gozo Island
Nearest town	Xaghra
Language spoken	Maltese, English, and Italian
Local currency	Euro
Average temperatures	46–59°F winter, 71–82°F summer
Vaccinations required	None
Type	Red sand
Dimensions	Length 800 yards, width 30 yards
Facilities	Kiosks, bar, sun lounger and sun umbrella rental
Suitable for families/kids	Yes
When to go	June to September

THE BEACH

Name	Ao Maya, known as The Beach
Country	Thailand
Region	Koh Phi Phi Leh Island
Nearest town	None
Language spoken	Thai
Local currency	Baht
Average temperatures	77–86°F
Vaccinations required	None
Type	Sand and high cliffs
Dimensions	Length around 300 yards, width 30 yards
Facilities	No
Suitable for families/kids	No
When to go	November to February

UTAH BEACH

Name	Utah Beach
Country	France
Region	Normandy
Nearest town	Sainte Marie du Mont
Language spoken	French
Local currency	Euro
Average temperatures	39–46°F winter, 60–68°F summer
Vaccinations required	None
Type	Sand
Dimensions	Length around 3 miles, width up to 100 yards
Facilities	No
Suitable for families/kids	No
When to go	May to September

VENICE LIDO

Name	Venice Lido
Country	Italy
Region	Veneto
Nearest town	Venice
Language spoken	Italian
Local currency	Euro
Average temperatures	39–43°F winter, 75–82°F summer
Vaccinations required	None
Type	Sand
Dimensions	Length 3 miles, width up to 100 yards
Facilities	Private beach areas with beach huts, hotel, refreshments
Suitable for families/kids	Yes
When to go	June to September

WAIKIKI

Name	Waikiki
Country	United States
Region	Hawaii
Nearest town	Honolulu
Language spoken	English with lots of Hawaiian words
Local currency	US dollar
Average temperatures	72–84°F
Vaccinations required	None
Type	Sand
Dimensions	Length 2 miles, width up to 800 yards
Facilities	Sports gear rental, private beach areas, refreshments
Suitable for families/kids	Yes
When to go	Year-round

AITUTAKI

Name	Aitutaki
Country	New Zealand
Region	Cook Islands
Nearest town	None
Language spoken	Maori and English
Local currency	NZ dollar
Average temperatures	79–82°F
Vaccinations required	None
Type	Fine sand
Dimensions	Length around 6 miles, along perimeter of island, width up to 30 yards
Facilities	At hotels
Suitable for families/kids	Yes
When to go	April to November

ANSE DE MAYS

Name	Anse de Mays
Country	France
Region	Guadeloupe
Nearest town	Saint-Louis
Language spoken	French
Local currency	Euro
Average temperatures	72–86°F
Vaccinations required	None
Type	Fine sand
Dimensions	Length around 500 yards, width 10 yards
Facilities	No
Suitable for families/kids	Yes
When to go	December to April

BANGARAM

Name	Bangaram
Country	India
Region	Kerala
Nearest town	None
Language spoken	Hindi
Local currency	Rupee
Average temperatures	77–90°F
Vaccinations required	None
Type	Sand, coral reef, palm trees
Dimensions	Length around 3 miles, around edge of island
Facilities	Only at resorts
Suitable for families/kids	Yes
When to go	November to March

BAYAHIBE

Name	Bayahibe
Country	Dominican Republic
Region	Southeast coast
Nearest town	La Romana
Language spoken	Spanish
Local currency	Dominican peso
Average temperatures	68–90°F
Vaccinations required	None
Type	White sand and cliffs
Dimensions	Length 6 miles, width around 20 yards
Facilities	Paid well-equipped sections with sun loungers, bar, private beach areas
Suitable for families/kids	Yes
When to go	December to May

BELLE MARE

Name	Belle Mare
Country	Mauritius
Region	Flacq
Nearest town	Flacq
Language spoken	English, French and Creole
Local currency	Mauritian rupee
Average temperatures	75–86°F
Vaccinations required	None
Type	Fine white sand
Dimensions	Length 3 miles, width up to 40 yards
Facilities	Only at hotels
Suitable for families/kids	Yes
When to go	Year-round

CABBAGE BEACH

Name	Cabbage Beach
Country	Bahamas
Region	New Providence
Nearest town	None
Language spoken	English
Local currency	Bahamian dollar
Average temperatures	70–82°F
Vaccinations required	None
Type	Fine white sand
Dimensions	Length 6 miles, width up to 50 yards
Facilities	Golf course, casino, aquarium, refreshments
Suitable for families/kids	Yes
When to go	Year-round

CALA VIOLINA

Name	Cala Violina
Country	Italy
Region	Tuscany
Nearest town	Grosseto
Language spoken	Italian
Local currency	Euro
Average temperatures	41–50°F winter, 73–82°F summer
Vaccinations required	None
Type	Fine sand, posidonia seaweed areas on sea floor
Dimensions	Length 300 yards, width up to 40 yards
Facilities	Just a few benches and tables
Suitable for families/kids	Yes
When to go	May to September

CORAL BAY

Name	Coral Bay
Country	Egypt
Region	Southern Sinai
Nearest town	Sharm El Sheikh
Language spoken	Arabic, Italian, English and Russian
Local currency	Egyptian pound
Average temperatures	68–86°F
Vaccinations required	None
Type	Sand, coral reef
Dimensions	Length 1 mile, width 40 yards
Facilities	Pontoons, diving center, and all facilities
Suitable for families/kids	Yes
When to go	April to June, September to November

CUA DAI

Name	Cua Dai
Country	Vietnam
Region	Quang Nam
Nearest town	Hoi An
Language spoken	Vietnamese
Local currency	Dong
Average temperatures	70–82°F
Vaccinations required	None
Type	Fine sand
Dimensions	Length over 6 miles, width up to 300 yards
Facilities	At Hotel Victoria
Suitable for families/kids	Yes
When to go	April to September

FRANCISQUI

Name	Francisqui
Country	Venezuela
Region	Los Roques
Nearest town	None
Language spoken	Spanish
Local currency	Bolivar
Average temperatures	79–88°F
Vaccinations required	None
Type	Sand, coral
Dimensions	Length 6 miles, width varies
Facilities	None
Suitable for families/kids	No
When to go	October to March

HERON ISLAND

Name	Heron Island
Country	Australia
Region	Queensland
Nearest town	None
Language spoken	English
Local currency	Australian dollar
Average temperatures	79–86°F
Vaccinations required	None
Type	Fine white sand
Dimensions	Length around 3 miles, along island perimeter, width up to 20 yards
Facilities	Yes
Suitable for families/kids	Yes
When to go	October to April

JHONNY CAY

Name	Jhonny Cay
Country	Colombia
Region	San Andrés
Nearest town	None
Language spoken	Spanish and English
Local currency	Colombian peso
Average temperatures	79–86°F
Vaccinations required	None
Type	Fine white sand
Dimensions	Length around 1 mile, width a dozen yards
Facilities	No
Suitable for families/kids	Yes
When to go	December to March

MANIHI

Name	Manihi
Country	French Polynesia
Region	Tuamotu Islands
Nearest town	Paeua
Language spoken	Tahitian English
Local currency	Central Pacific franc, euro, US dollar
Average temperatures	72–80°F; rain between December and March
Vaccinations required	None
Type	Marvelous sea and black pearl farms
Dimensions	Small atoll
Facilities	Dive center and refreshments
Suitable for families/kids	Yes
When to go	April to October

NGAPALI BEACH

Name	Ngapali Beach
Country	Myanmar
Region	Rakhine
Nearest town	Ngapali
Language spoken	Burmese
Local currency	Kyat
Average temperatures	86–90°F
Vaccinations required	None
Type	Fine sand
Dimensions	Length 3 miles, width 100 yards
Facilities	Only at resorts
Suitable for families/kids	Yes
When to go	November to April

DIANI BEACH

Name	Diani Beach
Country	Kenya
Region	Coast
Nearest town	Mombasa
Language spoken	Swahili and English
Local currency	Kenya Shilling
Average temperatures	75–95°F
Vaccinations required	Anti-malarial recommended
Type	White sand, fringed by palm trees and baobabs
Dimensions	Length 15 miles, width up to 50 yards
Facilities	Resort, bungalow and tourist facilities
Suitable for families/kids	Yes
When to go	April to May

GRANDE ANSE DES SALINES

Name	Grande Anse des Salines
Country	France
Region	Martinique - Overseas Department
Nearest town	None
Language spoken	French and Creole
Local currency	Euro
Average temperatures	72–82°F
Vaccinations required	None
Type	White sand
Dimensions	Length 1200 yards, width up to 20 yards
Facilities	Just a few kiosks with local food and drink, paid sun loungers
Suitable for families/kids	Yes
When to go	December to February

LE MORNE

Name	Le Morne
Country	Mauritius
Region	Le Morne Brabant
Nearest town	None
Language spoken	English, French, and Creole
Local currency	Rupee
Average temperatures	68–81°F, 39–88°F November to April
Vaccinations required	None
Type	Fine white sand
Dimensions	Length 4 miles, width up to 30 yards
Facilities	Only at resorts
Suitable for families/kids	Yes
When to go	March to December

PISCINAS

Name	Piscinas
Country	Italy
Region	Sardinia
Nearest town	Cagliari
Language spoken	Italian
Local currency	Euro
Average temperatures	46–54°F winter, 73–81°F summer
Vaccinations required	None
Type	Sand
Dimensions	Length 3 miles, width 100 yards
Facilities	Kiosks, canoe and inflatable rental, life guard
Suitable for families/kids	Yes
When to go	May to October

PONELOYA

Name	Poneloya
Country	Nicaragua
Region	León
Nearest town	León
Language spoken	Spanish
Local currency	Cordoba
Average temperatures	75–88°F
Vaccinations required	None
Type	Sand
Dimensions	Length 6 miles, width up to 500 yards
Facilities	Restaurant, hotels, surfboard rental
Suitable for families/kids	No
When to go	December to April

PWANI MCHANGANI

Name	Pwani Mchangani
Country	Tanzania
Region	Zanzibar
Nearest town	Stone Town
Language spoken	Swahili
Local currency	Tanzanian shilling
Average temperatures	75–86°F
Vaccinations required	Anti-malarial prophylaxis
Type	Fine white sand
Dimensions	Length 3 miles, width up to 100 yards
Facilities	Sun umbrellas, sun loungers and restaurants
Suitable for families/kids	Yes
When to go	December to February, June to October

SPIAGGIA ROSA

Name	Spiaggia Rosa or Cala di Roto
Country	Italy
Region	Sardinia
Nearest town	La Maddalena
Language spoken	Italian
Local currency	Euro
Average temperatures	46–59°F winter, 68–81°F summer
Vaccinations required	None
Type	Pink sand
Dimensions	Length 110 yards, width up to 30 yards
Facilities	Boardwalk for viewing beach
Suitable for families/kids	No
When to go	April to June

BONDI BEACH

Name	Bondi Beach
Country	Australia
Region	New South Wales
Nearest town	Sydney
Language spoken	English
Local currency	Australian dollar
Average temperatures	50–59°F May to September, 68–79°F October to April
Vaccinations required	None
Type	Fine white sand
Dimensions	Length half-mile, width up to 100 yards
Facilities	Bar, surfboard and wet suit rental
Suitable for families/kids	Yes
When to go	December to February

PRAIA DO GUNGA

Name	Praia do Gunga
Country	Brazil
Region	Alagoas
Nearest town	Maceió
Language spoken	Portuguese
Local currency	Real
Average temperatures	82–91°F
Vaccinations required	None
Type	Sand
Dimensions	Length 700 yards, width up to 300 yards
Facilities	Sun loungers, sun umbrellas, bar
Suitable for families/kids	Yes
When to go	September to May

SALECCIA

Name	Saleccia
Country	France
Region	Corsica
Nearest town	Saint Florent
Language spoken	French
Local currency	Euro
Average temperatures	45–54°F winter, 73–82°F summer
Vaccinations required	None
Type	Fine white sand
Dimensions	Length half-mile, width up to 200 yards
Facilities	No
Suitable for families/kids	Yes
When to go	July to September

WINEGLASS BAY

Name	Wineglass Bay
Country	Australia
Region	Tasmania
Nearest town	None
Language spoken	English
Local currency	Australian dollar
Average temperatures	37–52°F June to August, 62–73°F December to February
Vaccinations required	None
Type	Sand white
Dimensions	Length 1.5 miles, width up to 40 yards
Facilities	No
Suitable for families/kids	No
When to go	December to March

PRAIA POMBAS

Name	Praia Pombas
Country	São Tomé e Principe
Region	São Tomé Island
Nearest town	São Tomé
Language spoken	Portuguese and Creole
Local currency	Dobra
Average temperatures	77–86°F
Vaccinations required	Yellow fever essential. Cholera, viral hepatitis and malaria recommended
Type	Sand, fine
Dimensions	Length 500 yards, width around 15 yards
Facilities	No
Suitable for families/kids	Yes
When to go	December to February

SALINE

Name	Saline
Country	France
Region	Guadalupe – Overseas Department
Nearest town	Gustavia
Language spoken	French
Local currency	Euro
Average temperatures	72–86°F
Vaccinations required	None
Type	Sand
Dimensions	Length around 300 yards, width up to 30 yards
Facilities	No
Suitable for families/kids	No
When to go	December to April

ZLATNI RAT

Name	Zlatni Rat
Country	Croatia
Region	Dalmatia
Nearest town	Bol
Language spoken	Croat
Local currency	Kuna
Average temperatures	43–50°F winter, 75–82°F summer
Vaccinations required	None
Type	Small pebbles
Dimensions	Length 700 yards, width 250 yards
Facilities	Refreshments, cold showers and car park
Suitable for families/kids	Yes
When to go	May to September

CABARETE

Name	Cabarete
Country	Dominican Republic
Region	Puerto Plata
Nearest town	Cabarete
Language spoken	Spanish
Local currency	Dominican peso
Average temperatures	77–86°F
Vaccinations required	None
Type	White sand
Dimensions	Length 3 miles, width up to 100 yards
Facilities	Refreshments, cafés *chantants*, sun loungers, open-air gyms
Suitable for families/kids	Yes
When to go	January to March

CLIFTON BEACH

Name	Clifton Beach
Country	South Africa
Region	Western Cape
Nearest town	Cape Town
Language spoken	English
Local currency	South African rand
Average temperatures	66–75°F November to March, 50–57°F April to October
Vaccinations required	None
Type	Sand
Dimensions	Length half mile, width up to 50 yards
Facilities	Sun loungers, deckchairs, all services
Suitable for families/kids	Yes
When to go	November to March

EN VAU

Name	En Vau
Country	France
Region	Provence
Nearest town	Marseille
Language spoken	French
Local currency	Euro
Average temperatures	43–55°F winter, 68–79°F summer
Vaccinations required	None
Type	Sand and pebble
Dimensions	Length 40 yards, width 15 yards
Facilities	No
Suitable for families/kids	Yes
When to go	April to October

GRANDE PLAGE

Name	Grande Plage
Country	France
Region	Aquitaine
Nearest town	Biarritz
Language spoken	French and Basque
Moneta locale	Euro
Average temperatures	43–50°F winter, 59–68°F summer
Vaccinations required	None
Type	Sand
Dimensions	Length 500 yards, width 100 yards
Facilities	Sun loungers and umbrellas to rent, restaurants and bar
Suitable for families/kids	Yes
When to go	May to June

JERICOACOARA

Name	Jericoacoara
Country	Brazil
Region	Ceará
Nearest town	Parnaíba
Language spoken	Portuguese
Local currency	Brazilian real
Average temperatures	72–81°F
Vaccinations required	None
Type	Sand and large dunes
Dimensions	Length around 12 miles, width varies
Facilities	Tourist facilities, sports facilities
Suitable for families/kids	Yes
When to go	November to March

LE TOUQUET

Name	Le Touquet-Paris Plage
Country	France
Region	Nord-Pas-de-Calais
Nearest town	Le Touquet
Language spoken	French
Local currency	Euro
Average temperatures	33–43°F winter, 55–70°F summer
Vaccinations required	None
Type	Sand
Dimensions	Length 6 miles, width up to 300 yards
Facilities	Sports facilities, nautical facilities, water park, all services
Suitable for families/kids	Yes
When to go	April to November

MANGROVE BEACH

Name	Mangrove Beach
Country	Egypt
Region	Red Sea
Nearest town	Marsa Alam
Language spoken	Arabic, English, and Italian
Local currency	Egyptian pound
Average temperatures	64–77°F winter, 82–104°F summer
Vaccinations required	None
Type	Sand, rocks, and brush
Dimensions	Length 2 miles, width up to 50 yards
Facilities	Al fresco bar and public bathrooms
Suitable for families/kids	No
When to go	November to March

PLAYA TAMARINDO

Name	Playa Tamarindo
Country	Costa Rica
Region	Nicoya
Nearest town	Tamarindo
Language spoken	Spanish and English
Local currency	US dollars, euro
Average temperatures	77–90°F
Vaccinations required	None
Type	Fine sand
Dimensions	Length 2 miles, width up to 100 yards
Facilities	No
Suitable for families/kids	Yes
When to go	December to April

SOUTH BEACH

Name	South Beach
Country	United States
Region	Florida
Nearest town	Miami
Language spoken	English and Spanish
Local currency	US dollars
Average temperatures	61–73°F winter, 75–88°F summer
Vaccinations required	None
Type	White sand
Dimensions	Length around 3 miles, width up to 200 yards
Facilities	Sun loungers, sun umbrellas, bar
Suitable for families/kids	Yes
When to go	November to April

VENICE BEACH

Name	Venice Beach
Country	United States
Region	California
Nearest town	Los Angeles
Language spoken	English and Spanish
Local currency	US dollars
Average temperatures	54–61°F winter, 73–81°F summer
Vaccinations required	None
Type	Sand
Dimensions	Length 1.5 miles, width up to 200 yards
Facilities	Playing fields, skating area, open-air gym, cycling, and pedestrian trail
Suitable for families/kids	Yes
When to go	December to April

WAIMEA BAY

Name	Waimea Bay
Country	United States
Region	Hawaii – Oahu Island
Nearest town	Honolulu
Language spoken	English
Local currency	US dollars
Average temperatures	77–93°F
Vaccinations required	None
Type	Red sand
Dimensions	Length around 1 mile, width up to 50 yards
Facilities	Bar and various services
Suitable for families/kids	Yes
When to go	Year-round

ARRECIFES

Name	Arrecifes
Country	Colombia
Region	Magdalena
Nearest town	Santa Marta
Language spoken	Spanish
Local currency	Colombian peso
Average temperatures	77–86°F
Vaccinations required	None
Type	Fine sand and rounded boulders
Dimensions	7,400 acres of park
Facilities	Restaurants, beach huts, hammocks
Suitable for families/kids	No
When to go	December to March

BALOS

Name	Balos
Country	Greece
Region	Crete
Nearest town	Kissamos-Kastelli
Language spoken	Greek
Local currency	Euro
Average temperatures	50–57°F winter, 79–82°F summer
Vaccinations required	None
Type	Fine white sand
Dimensions	Length 600 yards, width up to 40 yards
Facilities	High season only, sun loungers and bar
Suitable for families/kids	Yes
When to go	April to November

BERIKNICA

Name	Beriknica
Country	Croatia
Region	Dalmatia – Pag Island
Nearest town	Metajina
Language spoken	Croat
Local currency	Kuna
Average temperatures	68–86°F May to September
Vaccinations required	None
Type	Pebble and cliffs
Dimensions	Length 700 yards, width up to 100 yards
Facilities	None
Suitable for families/kids	No
When to go	May to September

CALA CINQUE DENTI

Name	Cala Cinque Denti
Country	Italy
Region	Sicily
Nearest town	Trapani
Language spoken	Italian and Pantesco
Local currency	Euro
Average temperatures	48–57°F winter, 68–86°F summer
Vaccinations required	None
Type	Cliffs and rocks
Dimensions	Length 50 yards, width 20 yards
Facilities	No
Suitable for families/kids	No
When to go	May to October

GIROLATA

Name	Girolata
Country	France
Region	Corsica
Nearest town	Girolata village
Language spoken	French
Local currency	Euro
Average temperatures	45–54°F winter, 73–82°F summer
Vaccinations required	None
Type	Pebble
Dimensions	Length around 200 yards, width 30 yards
Facilities	No
Suitable for families/kids	Yes
When to go	May to September

LOVE AND DIVORCE BEACH

Name	Love and Divorce Beach
Country	Mexico
Region	Baja California
Nearest town	Cabo San Lucas
Language spoken	Spanish
Local currency	Mexican peso
Average temperatures	77–86°F
Vaccinations required	None
Type	Very fine sand
Dimensions	Length 30 yards, width 10 yards
Facilities	No
Suitable for families/kids	Yes
When to go	May to September

PALMETTO POINT

Name	Palmetto Point
Country	Barbuda
Region	Antigua and Barbuda
Nearest town	None
Language spoken	English
Local currency	Eastern Caribbean dollar
Average temperatures	79–86°F
Vaccinations required	None
Type	Sand
Dimensions	Length 6 miles, width up to 500 yards
Facilities	No
Suitable for families/kids	Yes
When to go	December to February

PUNTA PIRULIL

Name	Punta Pirulil
Country	Chile
Region	Isola Grande de Chiloé
Nearest town	Cucao
Language spoken	Spanish
Local currency	Chilean peso
Average temperatures	41–57°F April to October, 59–75 °F November to March
Vaccinations required	None
Type	Sand and pebble
Dimensions	Length 6 miles, width up to 100 yards
Facilities	No
Suitable for families/kids	No
When to go	November to March

QALANSYA

Name	Qalansya
Country	Yemen
Region	Island of Socotra
Nearest town	None
Language spoken	Arabic
Local currency	Yemeni Riyal
Average temperatures	77–86°F winter, up to 122°F summer
Vaccinations required	Anti-malarial prophylaxis recommended
Type	Fine sand
Dimensions	Length 6 miles, width up to 100 yards
Facilities	No
Suitable for families/kids	No
When to go	October to April

INDEX

Cover and art direction: Roberta Grossi
Editorial management: Valeria Grandi, Elisabetta Versace
Translation: Mary Hegarty
Layout: Edit Srl, Milano

Copyeditor: Sabrina Talarico
Photo editor: Franco Barbagallo, Viviana Buora

Writers and Photographers:

Fabrizio Angeloro, Marco Asprea, Adriano Bacchella, Franco Barbagallo, Stefano Bartoli, Cristina Berbenni, Matteo Beretta, Marco Bevilacqua, Maria Luisa Bonivento, Anna Borgoni, Fabio Bottonelli, Dario Bragaglia, Germana Cabrelle, Teresa Carrubba, Marco Casiraghi, Maurizio Cattaneo, Vincenzo Chierchia, Margherita Colnaghi, Enrico Maria Corno, Paolo Crespi, Maria Celestina Crucillà, Marco Dal Pian, Carmen Davolo, Adriana De Santis, Claudia Farina, Leonardo Felician, Marina Fracasso, Paolo Gerbaldo, Rosalba Graglia, Isa Grassano, Mimmo Jodice, Graziella Leporati, Luca Liguori, Donatella Luccarini, Majrani, Renato Malman, Evelina Marchesini, Nicoletta Martelletto, Ada Mascheroni, Pamela Mc Court Francescone, Roberto Miliacca, Marina Moioli, Angelo Mojetta, Claudio Mollo, Filippo Occhino, Giuseppe Ortolano, Stefano Passaquindici, Giancarlo Pessina, Elisabetta Pina, Elena Pizzetti, Gabriella Poli, Rosanna Precchia, Francesca Rebonato, Mauro Remondino, Maria Cristina Renis, Claudio Rizzi, Silvana Rizzi, Basilio Rodella, Carmen Rolle, Giancarlo Roversi, Cecilia Sgherza, Manuela Soressi, Beatrice Spagnoli, Edoardo Stucchi, Claudia Sugliano, Sabrina Talarico, Marco Tenucci, Christian Unterkircher, Laura Varalla, Gaetano Zoccali, Riccardo Zoppini.

First published in the United States of America in 2011
by Universe Publishing, a division of Rizzoli International Publications, Inc.
300 Park Avenue South, New York, NY 10010
www.rizzoliusa.com

Originally published in Italian as 100 *Spiagge da vedere nella vita* in 2010 by Rizzoli Libri Illustrati
© 2010 RCS Libri Spa, Milano
www.rizzoli.eu

Second printing, 2015
2015 2016 2017 2018 / 10 9 8 7 6 5 4 3 2

ISBN: 978-0-7893-2729-1
Library of Congress Catalog Control Number: 2013950506

Printed in China